PRAISE FOR ACRASSICAUDA
& HEAVY METAL IN BAGHDAD

What an awesome story. This inspires me a lot. In the world, certain cultures are the way they are but music doesn't care. There are no boundaries for music. It connects right here in your heart. You can't stop it. So, right on!

—JAMES HETFIELD, METALLICA

When I heard there was a heavy metal band in Baghdad, I was immediately interested to find out more. I instantaneously knew it would be a death-defying act to play any kind of rock 'n' roll music there, as rock is such a Western invention. I'd guess, as the rock gets harder sounding, it seems all the more insulting to the traditional Iraqi sensibility and that's what made Acrassicauda as much daredevil as inspirational. Music is my religion and I know that feeling of necessity that you get about playing music. The peace it brings to troubled minds. But I can't imagine the emotional endurance it'd take to risk death just to buy guitar strings.

For me, the story of Acrassicauda is such an important one because it's one of the few Iraqi stories I've heard of that is truly about freedom for Iraqi people. Theirs is an unknown war, fought in the middle of another.

Music explains thoughts and feelings difficult to express in any other way and, perhaps nowadays, music's miraculous impact is taken for granted . . . until you see something like this. It'll make you put down your emo CDs faster than you would a John Tesh Groundhog Day album. [The *Heavy Metal in Baghdad* documentary] should be mandatory viewing to any band who lip-synchs, pulls the status quo, or thinks it's been a while since they loved themselves.

—JOSH HOMME, QUEENS OF THE STONE AGE

Commitment and heart are things that are immeasurable from the outside perspective of the human experience. You simply cannot walk by someone and know what lies beneath the exterior. You have to look into their eyes, you have to hear their words, and you have to see how they react when times are hard.

Acrassicauda have a story that you cannot know. You cannot walk in their shoes. You cannot see through their eyes. Their story demands to be heard. You fucking owe them at least that much.

While in their heart and sound they walk beside Mastodon, Slayer, and the rest of us, in their spirit and soul they are much more akin to people like Malcolm X, Bobby Sands, and all people who stand up righteously in the face of tyrants.

—SCOTT KELLY, NEUROSIS

I first heard of Acrassicauda in the spring of 2008 via *Heavy Metal in Baghdad*. On watching the movie, any thoughts about my own "struggles" being a musician were quickly put to shame. Sure, I've dealt with my share of canceled flights, lost luggage, and equipment failure. But these guys have had to deal with bombings, curfews, sniper fire, and a country under occupation and on the verge of civil war. Their story proves that metal crosses all borders and that music and art should be supported by governments, not just donations from caring individuals and companies. The acts of pounding the drums, thumping the bass, making the guitars scream, yelling into the mike, and being on the receiving end as a listener provide a welcome respite from daily life. This is true whether you're a frustrated teen, safe in the suburbs of the U.S., or someone facing life-threatening dangers in a country such as Iraq. The guys in Acrassicauda value metal enough to face insurmountable odds just for the freedom of playing it.

—ALEX SKOLNICK, TESTAMENT

Watching *Heavy Metal in Baghdad* put things into perspective. You do tend to take things for granted when you just start and can go down in your practice space and it hasn't been hit by a bomb. I just felt bad that they had to go through all that just to rock, and it's such a nonissue here. The furthest thing from your mind would be that someone would try to stop you from it. I think they are incredibly courageous, and it obviously gave them the fuel to keep going.

I can't imagine being in that scenario at all. I don't have any point of reference for that. I wouldn't even pretend to say that I could empathize with that situation. So my heart went out to them, and I hope that I get to meet them sometime. It's a very inspiring story.

—BRANN DAILOR, MASTODON

The film gives Westerners an unadulterated view into a world where simple freedoms such as playing thrash metal are punishable by death.

The story of Acrassicauda gives us an opportunity not just to follow the lives of these four metalheads but also to get a better insight into what kind of freedoms and luxuries are not available in that part of the world, and maybe even how we, as a free country, take these gifts for granted. I support this film not only as a metalhead myself but also as a human being.

—JOE TROHMAN, FALL OUT BOY

Both a stirring testament to the plight of cultural expression in Baghdad and a striking report on the refugee scene in Syria, this rock-doc like no other electrifies its genre and redefines headbanging as an act of hardcore courage.

—*THE NEW YORK TIMES*

More than just another Iraq-doc, *Heavy Metal* is a surprisingly up-close look at the toll of the war on young people, and how they still have dreams and still want to jam, party, and get down. If *Once* was about the romance of creativity, *Heavy Metal in Baghdad* is about the total, unrelenting obsession. They have no choice. They must rock.

—THE LOS ANGELES TIMES

Western metal acts are bound to feel like poseurs when they see this intense documentary on Acrassicauda . . . the dangers these musicians experience every single day are bound to impact any audience. This is what it really looks like to bang your head against the wall.

—NEW YORK DAILY NEWS

The movie reclaims metal's appeal to the powerless as well as its threat—when you can get shot for wearing a Slipknot T-shirt . . . or speaking the English you learned off *Master of Puppets*, raising those devil horns isn't an empty act of aggression.

—VILLAGE VOICE

There is a genuine poignancy in the way these brash young men find the determination to endure through Slayer and Slipknot. You can only wonder how a gravely wounded people can survive a nation's demise.

—TIME OUT NEW YORK

Whether you love or hate metal, Acrassicauda's struggle to stay together—and alive—will rock you.

—NEWSWEEK

A great parable about rock 'n' roll as an act of brotherhood and faith in collective survival.

—NEW YORK SUN

[An] urgent movie about choices that are entitlements to some but unimaginable luxuries for others.

—THE NEW YORKER

HEAVY METAL

THE STORY OF ACRASSICAUDA

BY ANDY CAPPER & GABI SIFRE

ACRASSICAUDA

Faisal Talal
Tony Aziz
Firas Al-Lateef
& Marwan Riyadh

IN BAGHDAD

MTV | BOOKS

POCKET BOOKS
New York   London   Toronto   Sydney

HEAVY METAL IN BAGHDAD
The Story of Acrassicauda
By Andy Capper and Gabi Sifre
Editorial Assistance by Tim Small
Transcriptions by Bruno Bayley, Andrew Chadwick, James Knight, Gabi Sifre,
Alexander Dunbar, and Ryan Bradford.
All photos courtesy of the band unless otherwise marked.
Previous spread: Acrassicauda playing at Kemanci Club, Istanbul, Turkey, 2008.
Photo by Ahmet Polat.

Pocket Books
A Division of Simon & Schuster, Inc.
1230 Avenue of the Americas
New York, NY 10020

First MTV Books/Pocket Books trade paperback edition November 2009

POCKET and colophon are registered trademarks of Simon & Schuster, Inc.

For information about special discounts for bulk purchases, please contact Simon &
Schuster Special Sales at 1-866-506-1949 or business@simonandschuster.com

The Simon & Schuster Speakers Bureau can bring authors to your live event. For
more information or to book an event contact the Simon & Schuster Speakers Bureau
at 1-866-248-3049 or visit our website at www.simonspeakers.com.

Designed by Evil Twin Publications

Manufactured in the United States of America

10 9 8 7 6 5 4 3 2 1

Library of Congress Cataloging-in-Publication Data is available.

ISBN 978-1-4165-9540-3
ISBN 978-1-4391-2684-4 (ebook)

Dedicated to the Tak Machi Building, Karadah,
our first practice space, where everything started.

↗ CONTENTS ↖

"Nobody was expecting that in Iraq heavy metal could exist...
We started it and we're not gonna stop." —Acrassicauda

HEAVY METAL
IN BAGHDAD

حفي بتل إن بغداد

BERLIN
INTERNATIONAL
FILM FESTIVAL
OFFICIAL SELECTION
2008

TORONTO
INTERNATIONAL
FILM FESTIVAL
OFFICIAL SELECTION
2007

VBS.TV PRESENTS A VICE FILMS PRODUCTION "HEAVY METAL IN BAGHDAD" A FILM BY EDDY MORETTI AND SUROOSH ALVI MUSIC BY ACRASSICAUDA EDITED BY BERNARDO LOYOLA
EXECUTIVE PRODUCERS SHANE SMITH AND SPIKE JONZE PRODUCED BY MONICA HAMPTON PRODUCED AND DIRECTED BY EDDY MORETTI AND SUROOSH ALVI

WWW.HEAVYMETALINBAGHDAD.COM

VICE FILMS   VBS.TV

AN
INTRODUCTION
TO
ACRASSICAUDA

(pronounced A-Crass-I-Cowda)

I first met the Iraqi heavy metal band Acrassicauda in Istanbul. It was the summer of 2008 and I was there to conduct the first interviews that would go toward this book.

Over four days I recorded about thirty-six hours of conversation, and that makes up the lion's share of what you will go on to read.

We talked mostly on the rooftop terrace of the Grand Hotel de Londres, a 1930s-style colonial English hotel in downtown Istanbul, but also in the back of speeding taxicabs, in noisy, smoky cafés, and at their various abodes in the run-down parts of town where refugees were sent to live by the government. Over that week, I would get to know Marwan, Faisal, Firas, and Tony quite well and my perceptions of them changed quite dramatically.

I first heard their story when I edited the first-ever *Vice* article about them that we ran in the Obsessions Issue, written by Gideon Yago, and as much as the story and the resulting movie that Vice Films released in 2007 affected me, nothing would prepare me for hearing their stories face-to-face.

Hearing about the brutality of American foreign policy from some-body who's roughly the same age and social class and has the same record collection as you is a lot more affecting than hearing it from somebody wearing a suit sitting behind a news desk.

Hearing their stories in detail and going back over them again and again to edit them made me realize that their story is not really about heavy metal, nor is it really about Baghdad. It's about what happens to people when their lives are blown to smithereens by the world and how they adapt, cope, survive, and recover.

Personally, I sometimes read it like a self-help manual.

Ladies and gentlemen, I give you . . . Acrassicauda.

—*Andy Capper,* Vice *magazine, London*

HEAVY METAL IN BAGHDAD

هﭪﻲ ﭥﻞ إن بغداد

ACRASSICAUDA

WELCOME TO A
HARD ROCK & HEAVY METAL
LIVE CONCERT

تقام الحفلة في (نادي الهندية)

كراج خارج

DATE .... / ...... / 2004
TIME ...... ۳:۰۰ P.M

باع الطـ........

AND DON'T FORGET
IT'S HAPPEN ONLY IN A LIFE TIME
SO DON'T MISS IT

WELCOME TO THE REAL
WORLD

FLYER FOR A SHOW AT THE HINDYA CLUB ON JANUARY 5, 2004, BAGHDAD.

ROOTS BLOODY ROOTS

FIRAS AL-LATEEF (bass): I was born in Baghdad. My family is totally Iraqi. We are Muslims and we don't believe in differences between religions or sects.

I have one brother and one sister. I grew up in a middle-class neighborhood. My father is a doctor, a vet.

Sometimes I got to hang out with him at the surgery. Since I was a little kid, I used to go to the clinic and treat the animals. So I got a lot of experience with treating pets and stuff. We had a farm outside the city that we used to go to a couple of times a year. It's not really a farm, just a piece of land with animals and stuff.

MARWAN RIYADH (drums): My dad used to be in the military. He retired in 1988 after the Iranian war. My mum was a schoolteacher, and we're a pretty small family, an educated family. I'm the youngest one; I have two sisters.

What with my dad being in the military and my mother being a teacher, my family was strict. We had our issues with discipline in the house, mostly when I was a kid growing up. My mother was a headmistress in a school and she was worried about discipline in a school with three hundred fifty to four hundred students. So imagine when she'd come home and had to raise a family with my dad trying to pay off the bills with his small pension. They had high standards, and they were concerned about us getting a good education and how it would help us in the future. They paid for my sisters and stuff, for college. But I was kind of the ugly duckling of the family. I was a rebel and I was seeing the way life was and how education didn't really matter in my environment. It was all about money. I felt like I was living in a total paradox. That affected me within.

TONY AZIZ (lead guitar): My mum is a housekeeper; my father was in the army when he was younger. He was a war prisoner during the Iran-Iraq war for eleven years. So I was raised by a single mother with three sisters and one brother. I was the oldest. We lived in a house that we shared with another family. My dad came back in the nineties and is retired now; he's sixty years old. My mother is retired, too. They both live in Syria now. I was thirteen when my father came back from the war in Iran. Eventually, I would go on to join the Iraqi army as well. It was every Iraqi guy's destiny because it was mandatory. Considering the amount of wars Iraq had, it was a bit frightening to enlist.

FAISAL TALAL (vocals/guitar): My family was middle class. About seventy-five percent of people there used to work as officers or em-

FIRAS, FRIEND, MARWAN, TONY, AND FAISAL
AT THE PRACTICE SPACE IN BAGHDAD, 2004.

ployees for the government, but my dad wasn't much of a career guy. He worked many jobs. He was a teacher back when we used to live in Saudi Arabia—I was born there, my brothers and me. My father lived there for twenty-one years and my mother for about fourteen years, in a very small southern town. He taught English and my mother was a housekeeper.

We came to Iraq after the Gulf War. We were afraid that after the war, Saudi Arabia would not accept all of the Iraqis, so my father said, "Let's get out of here with our pride, without tears on our faces, before somebody says something to us." The funny thing was, after the war I was thinking, Oh good, so that's everything now. It's finished. It's going to be peacetime for Iraq. But then in 1990, the Gulf War began.

Because I was a kid, I would hear rumors about what was going to happen. My parents would tell me to be inside the house at 9:00 P.M. because it wasn't safe outside, but I wasn't quite sure about that.

The idea of war was not very comprehensible to me because I'd never experienced it before. Not like Marwan and Tony. Marwan's dad had been in the Iran-Iraq war, and Tony grew up in circumstances like that, too, what with his dad being in the military.

FIRAS: I wasn't a great student, but I kept things balanced—work, music, and studying. Where we grew up, you have to manage things from when you're a kid. You have to work and struggle to make your future. Some people don't agree with the idea of little kids working, but I think it builds a stronger personality. A kid who works will be in contact with a lot of older people, all sorts of people, he'll gain a lot of knowledge and a lot of strength—mental strength—as well as life experience. For us, the idea is not to earn money as much as to learn. Since I was ten or something I started working. Before that, any work I did was for free.

MARWAN: I started working when I was eleven years old, making sun seed bags. They're like sunflower seeds; you know, you'd get a book and rip out the pages and make bags of sunflower seeds, and sell them in dozens, for nickels. I didn't stop working until I was twenty-one and I left Iraq.

Then I started making falafel, and later started baking different things at home to sell. In Iraq you do whatever it takes so you can finish school and afford living, so I needed to do all I could. I started working in the neighborhood store, like from 6:00 to 7:30 A.M., help the milk guy unload, then I'd go to my school, come back at 2:00 P.M. and keep working until 9:00 or 10:00 at night. Then I started working in a video game store, then making leather bags and shoes in a factory. Bit by bit, I was going up the ladder and getting better jobs and salaries. I also worked as the editor of an Internet newspaper and at a music store. I don't remember now exactly, everything is so hazy, it feels like living someone else's life. But I was also taking the experience from previous jobs and sometimes what I learned in school.

One of the jobs I also had and was into was painting and drawing pictures for people. I drew all kinds of stuff. I used to paint for myself different things that came from my imagination, things that were living in my mind. I used coals all the time; I never liked to draw using colors. One of the happy memories I have of old Baghdad is going to the Almotanabi Street market every Friday morning [Friday is the Sabbath for Muslims], where they sold art supplies and comic books.

Drawing became the main problem I had with my parents. I'd open a book and instead of studying, I'd start to fill the corners and in between the lines with drawings. So in all of my schoolbooks, there are drawings of whatever I observed or was on my mind. My family thought I was reading but I wasn't. At that time, drawing was my only getaway from reality. So at that point, when the burdens of life started getting heavier, I tried to make the world inside my head a reality. That was my only sanctuary. I started drawing on the walls and ceiling. I was becoming more isolated, living through painting. I was interested in history and mythology, and I drew Tutankhamun, the pyramids, and gargoyles all over the walls. I didn't have enough big paper to draw on. It wasn't enough for how much I wanted to extend beyond all the burdens in my life. I didn't think anyone did. I couldn't afford my painting addiction.

At first my parents encouraged my drawing, then I started getting obsessed with it. That's when they stopped because it started affecting my school and getting out of control and all over the walls.

FIRAS: My father wanted me to be a vet, to carry on the legacy, but I didn't like it, not as a profession. When I was really young, my dream was to be a pilot. Then I grew up and opened my eyes. Your dreams don't change as you grow up, they kind of just get more realistic. To be a pilot you had to do math and I couldn't do math so there was no way. Plus, I wear glasses.

I'd always been fascinated with planes, though.

Anyway, my dream started as a pilot, then to become an engineer, then after high school I thought about going to art school, then I thought art school in our country doesn't mean much because you can't get a job with it. Then I thought about business administration. I had one year of college in Baghdad doing that. And I actually loved it. I love things where you get to meet people; it's not about being smart but more about calculating what you do. I know I suck at math, but I did great at college because in the banking system it's a different kind of math. You have a calculator, that makes it easier.

MARWAN: I wasn't bad at school, but the main reason for me having low grades was that the school was going downhill and it was impossible to bribe the teachers. Yeah, it sounds weird, but that's the way it was. You either had to study all the time, buy the teachers stuff, or take personal lessons to get good grades. I couldn't afford to buy them anything or take lessons, and I couldn't afford low grades, either. If your level was in between good and bad they'd just crush you down, and sometimes there was just no way to get your grades up. School began to feel like a dead end. Power was constantly cutting out at home. I used to go to the college near my house and ask the guard to turn on the field lights so we could sit on the benches and study.

Life was primitive down there when it came to power supplies, clean water, and even the markets. Every time you wanted to do anything, power would cut out and you'd have to light candles. It wasn't easy at all.

Boys like to hang out and mess around. There wasn't much to do besides soccer or smoking cigarettes on the corner behind the teachers' backs. The girls, they think it's their only chance maybe to get out of this life, so they work harder. But boys, they mess up once, and they are doomed. Some teachers were really not into their jobs and took out their frustrations on the students; some teachers were decent and went by the book. The hiring standards were very low. I tried so hard, but drawing too much was my main problem, plus I was working around ten hours a day. I didn't stop because I couldn't afford to. If I stopped for even one week that was it, I couldn't afford to go to school the next day. My family was too proud to admit that we couldn't support ourselves financially. That was worse mentally and emotionally for them; having to put on this mask of denial was a lot of pressure.

When it came time that I graduated from high school, I had a choice. Either finish another three years, go to college, and earn a degree, or go to an institute, study for five years, and get a teacher's diploma. I told my parents that I wanted to go to art school because I loved drawing, but the main reason for me was that I couldn't afford to go to college. But with fine art, it was easier, because I had it in me.

My family told me to finish high school and didn't accept the fact that I might not get a college degree. The whole idea freaked them out. My older sisters were bright and in college, and they wanted me to be like them. So I went back for another year and I failed, because I didn't want to be there and I wasn't happy doing it. It was like a two-semester nightmare. So my parents told me to stop going to work, they said they could pay for me. But I couldn't face telling them that the dinars they were giving me were not even nearly enough. They would work so hard to give me this amount of money, which I would then blow by failing the semester. It was twenty-five dinars to go to school and that would buy you a ticket on the bus, and I had to take two buses. Then I had to walk like two more kilometers.

So it was kind of tough, but after that I went to art school. I studied down there for five years; I dropped one year because I had to work. My work required fourteen or fifteen hours a day, so it was hard to go back and forth. But the work paid well. And then I had the band and practice, which is six or seven hours a day. There was not enough time to work, study, and play music, and music was always my priority.

FIRAS: My family wasn't musical, they weren't supportive really, but they didn't mind as long as it didn't affect my life as a student.

My brother and sister used to listen to Pink Floyd and hard rock and stuff, like . . . stoner style. I didn't know what the hell Pink Floyd was or what rock was, but my favorite album was *Dark Side of the Moon*. I used to sit and listen to it over and over. I didn't know what *Dark Side of the Moon* meant, or what kind of music it was, it was just music to me. So then I got the earliest albums, like *Animals*.

I didn't even know the names of the guys in the bands I used to like: I didn't know the band members or what types of music they played or what instruments they played. I listen to a lot of bands now and I still don't know all that stuff, because there are so many groups that I like and listen to.

I had *Dark Side of the Moon* on cassette and a little half-broken tape player. Whenever it broke I fixed it myself. Since that time, I liked the loudness and stuff, and at that time I wasn't speaking English, but I was starting through my dad. He speaks English and like five different languages, and he's been all around the world, so pretty much the way I grew up, I'd say it was like European, open-minded. The policy of my dad was "Do whatever you want but let me know when you get in trouble, so I can help you." That was the major rule. I had my own life and I did all sorts of stuff. And by that time I was much more into this death metal band called Sabbath.

It was hard to find metal records in Baghdad, but when I went to learn guitar I met people through my teacher, and these people have connections.

TONY: When I was four or five years old, I started listening to music. I listened to all kinds of stuff, like Michael Jackson, Pet Shop Boys, pop music. I got quite influenced by my cousins and other relatives who were older than me. That's how I started listening to music. When I was a kid I bought my first guitar but there was nobody to teach me. I was like five, six years old. It was a small guitar, made in China or something. I kept listening to music, and in the nineties I started listening to rock and metal, and reading about it, too, in magazines like *Metal Maniacs* and *Metal Age*. And the more I listened to rock and metal, the more I realized that was my favorite kind of sound. Life was hard, growing up in our environment. I was the oldest brother so I had to take more responsibility. Seeing my mother working as a housekeeper, I had to go out and find a source of income. I worked at a bakery and selling stuff on the street. The idea of my sisters working wasn't acceptable to me because they were younger. I wanted to take care of them.

FAISAL: My family led a very simple life: We didn't have that much influence from music except through listening to the radio.

My dad used to listen to jazz, but he left that when he got married and got all these responsibilities. It didn't make me interested in jazz music as much as it did in the drums. I begged my dad to get me a set and one day he bought me these little toy drums. After that day my dad spent a lot of time saying things to me like, "Shit, Faisal! I'm trying to sleep." Shortly, the drums disappeared. I still don't know what happened to them.

FIRAS: I didn't buy my own guitar until I got to learn bass, then I bought the bass guitar. My first guitar was an Aria Pro II. From that day on, I suppose the seeds of Acrassicauda were sown.

The Holy Lie

Forsaken through the endless Lands
I roam
The ripped our pride off and
Then they Asked for More
But forever more i'll stand my
ground
i'll carve my name entomB my
pain In every stone
~~I am your pain, fear~~
an evile King spread his wings
so wide
across The Lands Justifies his
Holy Lie
desert your life deny your needs
embrace the sin's to feed his
greed

2

CHILDREN OF THE GRAVE

FAISAL: When I was growing up there was no metal scene, but there were older guys listening to rock, like Deep Purple and Black Sabbath. There was nothing apart from simple pop music like A-Ha and stuff. Before he got into metal, my brother, Naif, was influenced by A-Ha and E-17.*

I had to listen to that kind of stuff for a time because I was sharing a room with my brother, so every time I woke up or he was studying, that's all I could hear. When he went to the record store,

*Editor's note: For some readers, it should be pointed out that E-17 was a council estate boy band from East London that did songs like "Everybody in the House of Love" and "Steam," which had really raunchy lyrics like "Outside it's raining but inside it's wet."

FAISAL AND SAAD ZAI POSING WITH SAAD'S ALBUM, BAGHDAD, IRAQ.

I had to join him and see who all the new bands were. I wasn't as attentive to music as I am now, but I liked it a lot.

MARWAN: I got into music when I was a kid. My dad bought me my first guitar when I was very little. I remember it was green. My family was really into Western music. My dad liked Dean Martin and Frank Sinatra, jazz and symphony music, as well as the older Arabic stuff. The first drum solo I saw that really made me want to play was by Buddy Rich.

Aside from what I listened to with my family, I started to develop my own tastes. Arabic music, then of course I got into Michael Jackson, then boy bands and New Age music, like Enigma and Enya. Then we listened to nineties rap music, like Tupac. I picked up my dad's interest in symphonies and kept that going. I think I had a rich musical blend.

Eventually I started listening to rock music, then metal, and I'm still exploring my musical tastes. Like sometimes listening to Bach or Vivaldi or a bit of jazz like Miles Davis or Louis Armstrong, or even traditional Iraqi music like Nazim Al-Ghazali or Makams. I don't have a limit; I listen to everything and I believe it helps me either way: It's like a win-win situation. I believe this is the best way to get into metal, by starting off with other music before delving in, because when people start listening to metal at an early age they still haven't got the whole concept of music—they look at it from a totally different perspective. By the time I started listening to metal, I'd been through all kinds, being from an Eastern background and getting attached to Western music. I think that gives you a certain appreciation of a variety of styles.

FAISAL: It was around the time that we came to Iraq that I started to figure what my future was going to be like. I began to listen to music in a really strong way. I used to listen to one or two songs a day and now I was listening to whole records. I was about eleven and it was 1995. The records were not just E-17—now it was stuff like Michael Jackson and Ace of Base. I was really into Michael Jackson and I would copy all his moves. Jackson was really big in Baghdad, like a lot of other foreign music. We had competitions at high school and we'd enter them to see who was the best Michael Jackson impersonator. I liked his songs. I also learned my English from him and many other bands. I would memorize all the lyrics and on the pirate videos we would buy from the black market stores in the city, I would watch the way he would talk to the audience at concerts. Iraqi parents can be strict, but my folks didn't really care too much about my Michael Jackson phase. It's not like they didn't care about me—it was just like, "He's a kid, he doesn't have to face the future now. He has a very long road to take, but he doesn't have to be a man tomorrow morning, or now." They always told me that I had to choose my way somehow. They showed me that I would have to be responsible for my mistakes and that someday maybe I was going to have to face something big.

I was not a show-off, but at the same time I imagined myself sometimes as different. I made a lot of friends at school listening to foreign music, because I had a lot to share with other people. I was always like, "Hey, you've got to listen to this. Have you ever heard that album? You've got to listen to this, come on!"

And I just kept hitting this on and on, and after three or four years, I just thought, How long am I going to keep doing this like an idiot?

FIRAS: Music was like an outlet for me, especially as a teenager and also now that I'm a grown man. Teenagers go through a lot of rough times and it helped me expel a lot of negative energies. The ones that I liked were mostly Pink Floyd and stuff, basically what my brother and sister were into. I used to listen to all kinds of English-speaking music. Then I started playing, and I started looking up styles and stuff like that.

Like, "Okay, this band is styled this [way], this is heavy metal, this is rock, this is pop-sounding, or this is hard rock." So I wasn't just like anybody. Then I started playing, and then through my music practice or basic knowledge I started to recognize different styles of music. I think pretty much every rocker in the world started like that.

FAISAL: Around that time, [my brother] Naif came up with the idea of playing guitar. He got them from friends, different ones, classicals, acoustics, and electrics. I had my eyes on the bass guitars. It wasn't that it was easier than guitar, but every one of my brother's friends that turned up would play a guitar, and I thought, Nobody's playing

PRACTICING FOR THE FIRST SHOW IN BAGHDAD, CIRCA 2001.

bass guitar. Sometimes they were in bands, heavy metal bands, rock and glam rock groups, even classical groups.

The eighties period had a very strange effect on my brother's generation, what with the haircuts and stuff. It was like he had the whole jungle on his head. He'd wear normal clothes because we don't have these multicolored eighties costumes and stuff like in the States. Plus he had to go to school. It was not a very good way to deal with school by going in supercolorful costumes. He wasn't in a band, but after years he started forming a classical music band, and after that he quit because he got married. Despite everything that happened, I never even thought about quitting.

So I started discovering new bands. At first it was things like the Backstreet Boys, but I got into harder stuff eventually. But it was still 1996, and back then I was into boy bands.

I liked this style at the time. We were in Iraq and, like I said before, we had very little exposure to the world of music and arts.

At some point, I developed the idea of forming a group by myself and that idea developed into maybe creating something with like four or five members. I wanted to start working as a team; I didn't want to work by myself. So we started forming all these groups.

We had a radio station called the V.O.Y.—it was Baghdad youth radio and it was very motivating; it used to broadcast a lot of famous songs and we would jam to them, so I got a group of friends together to dance and mime to the songs with and we called it Hello V.O.Y. We had this silly logo that was like a Mickey Mouse hand with four fingers waving. God, what were we thinking?

MARWAN: I was sixteen years old when Waleed Rabia and I started the whole idea of a boy band called Bad Boys. Everyone was making groups because of the V.O.Y. FM channel, the Voice of Youth channel, plus we were teenagers at that time. We wanted to do something but we didn't know what. It was a good way to connect with other young people because we were getting cut off from the outside world and the music community in Iraq and we just did not know how to meet other people with our same interests.

At that point, we didn't even have performing in mind because back then it wasn't something we imagined ourselves doing yet. I had known Waleed for about three years prior to that and when we got to high school we became close friends because we both had an interest in the English language and songs, too. We had kind of similar backgrounds, musical tastes, and depths of imagination, so we became good friends. He was into all the Voice of Youth stuff and then it was like a breeding ground or an epidemic, everyone started forming groups and that was how everyone from all of these different areas of Baghdad started connecting with each other.

WALEED RABIA (ex-Acrassicauda vocalist): The V.O.Y. radio station was very important to us at that time. I would ring up and request songs for girls I had never met in my life. Songs from people like Backstreet Boys, Five, and Boyzone. Yeah, it was the silly days. But I owe lots to these bands because I got to learn quite a bit of English listening to their lyrics.

Stuff like the word "drowning." I didn't know what it meant before but the boy bands would sing about "drowning in your love." So I would memorize the words in my head and I learned better English that way. In Bad Boys, we would give ourselves nicknames like "Bloodmaster." Marwan was "the Sorceror." We were the dictators of the band. We told the others what to do.

I met Marwan when he was having a fight with somebody and I was standing there looking and I watched as Marwan beat the other guy up. I was really enjoying it. Afterward I went up to him and said, "I really liked the way you fought the guy. I respect that." He said, "Who the hell are you?" but we ended up as friends. We would reign terror on our classmates. We would fight people in groups and we would keep fighting until we were out of breath. We usually won.

High schools back home are a rough place to be. There are lots of bullies and lots of fights. You don't want to be taken advantage of, so the idea is to go up to the toughest guy you can find and have a fight with him. The street laws are very firm. In Iraq you have to abide by the laws of the people. Stuff like, "If you don't want to get your ass kicked, don't harass any girls." If you get caught by their brothers, there can be some really severe consequences. Generally, if you go out to be a troublemaker you can end up in a lot of trouble yourself. I was a troublemaker myself—I tried to be a very good boy but it didn't work out. I'm still standing.

In Bad Boys, Marwan was the rapper and I would sing. Marwan was also a good dancer. He would bring the music videos and we would learn the moves. We would go to parties and do our dances. Oh my God, it's so embarrassing. "Backstreet's back! All right!" And we used to do a song by Five and it turned out good. I think Marwan will probably hate me forever if he heard me saying this, now that we're all metalheads and shit.

MARWAN: Doing Bad Boys was a way to fit in at school. We got way popular, whereas before we were just like geeks, with everyone picking on us every miserable day, which is why we had to fight. We were like outsiders; we did not get along with a lot of people at school. There were different groups: the kids who worried about wearing the right clothes and being on time with the fashions, and the kids who worried about getting good grades all the time, and the kids who didn't worry about anything at all. At that point, I was out of money. I remember I was between working selling falafels and making paintings, and I also used to work in a supermarket, but that was not even enough. Kids are just confused at that age—I kind of tried to fit in, but also I was just into the stuff I was into: painting and comics and whatever. Waleed was into the stuff I was doing and I was interested in the songs he was into, so we started liking the same things, the same pop bands. We'd rap and DJ and dance and we'd make art and flyers for the performances and it was fun. For me, it was about being with my friends, doing what I love the most, like making art and flyers and just listening to songs, and hanging out after school. Those were the good old days.

FAISAL: One time, when I was about fifteen, we went to the BIS [Baghdad International School] because they had these bazaars and DJ parties. They happened like twice a year. We needed to go there to see other people and other groups. We went there and had to face it, there was a lot of competition. That night we had to cover a lot of songs. The DJ would pick a song and they'd choose which group would dance to it and they'd just show off.

I never saw a girl dance, because it draws a lot of attention in our community. It's not like they don't do it, but not in public. I don't regret it because I'm going to have the silly naive memories for the rest of my life.

We copied the singing and dancing from every single video we could. Not MTV, just recorded cassettes. There were these video recording stores, and they'd be like, "I have the new video from Backstreet Boys, or the new concert from them," and we'd copy them from there. There was a neighborhood in Baghdad called the East Door [in the city center], and they had these huge stores that sold videos and electronics and stuff like that. We'd go in there all the time and get everything we could find that was connected to the music that we liked. Sometimes they'd have these shitty breaks in the tape so we had to cut and tape them back together. We'd save our pocket money and spend it all on these tapes.

There were about fifty or sixty groups with five or eight members each in Baghdad at that time, and they all had the same interest, the whole boy band thing.

WALEED: There was a school in Baghdad for internationals and they would have a public market, happenings, and food, and on Friday they would have a party with DJs.

They would only let couples in, so for single guys it was hard. I would go and meet girls and befriend them so we could go to these parties. When you got to the party, you would meet other groups that were in the same style as Bad Boys. This is how we met Faisal.

FAISAL: I guess you have to kind of get yourself updated after a while; you start thinking, Okay, this is the time that you have to change, go to the next step. And the next step was Metallica.

Well, before Metallica I listened to a bit of Bon Jovi and Scorpions and Bryan Adams, for some reason. My group kept listening to boy bands, but I was moving myself into other kinds of styles. And this is how I met Marwan.

What made me and Marwan even closer was that we would speak to each other in English. And I would go and hang out in his neighborhood. His was way chilled and mine was more like a prison. We just hung out and listened to music.

MARWAN: After a while, Waleed and I stopped Bad Boys because it was like, "That's all the fun you can get out of it." We then separated because I went to fine art school and that is when I started writing songs—I didn't have the idea of a band or anything, I was just writing because it was another artistic field for me to learn about. Waleed somehow got hooked up with Faisal through friends; I believe Faisal's brother and some of his friends were in a band. Faisal was very influenced by them; he was trying to play bass at that time and in the meantime I was changing my influences. I was listening to Sepultura, Scorpions, Anthrax, Metallica. The first Sepultura album I heard was *Roots*. I was at my friend's house with Waleed listening to it. You need to understand that there was no war at that point, but there was a big amount of social frustration going on for me, so metal was an avenue. And the first live concert I saw on video was Anthrax. I was surprised people could use that much foul language in a concert.

I was still growing up and going through different phases. I was thinking of these guys who put you down, the sickness that comes from working a full-time job, not being paid enough money, living in a middle-class community but living beneath any classes, and seeing your family struggling and things disappearing from the house because they were being sold. The economy was really weak because Iraq was under siege, so not a lot of stuff was coming into the country, like medical supplies and food. My dad had been retired since 1988 and there was not enough income. When you don't have enough money, mentally that will break you.

TONY: In the nineties I was mostly into glam rock, and stuff like Meatloaf and Mötley Crüe. Then I started working with music. I got record players and cassettes and magazines and started to sell them at the city center bazaar. Then around 1997, I decided that I should play some music. I started to look for a teacher but I couldn't find one until a year later. I studied with him for a short period and then I exchanged teachers for another one. After a short period, I stopped taking lessons from the second teacher. Around 2000, I found a guy named Saad Zai. He started teaching me, and I almost finished the whole program, and a year later I went out in concert with Acrassicauda, my first live show.

Having a band was always my dream. Being able to make music, just like the bands we used to see and hear. Also, rock was so inspiring for all of us, because it talks about different issues that people have in their daily life and it's not limited to one thing. It feels larger than life.

TOP: AT THE PRACTICE SPACE, BAGHDAD, 2003.
BOTTOM: MARWAN AND FIRAS AT THE PRACTICE SPACE, 2004.
MARWAN'S ART CAN BE SEEN IN THE BACKGROUND.

3

BORN
TO
RAISE HELL

FAISAL: I started to learn English by watching black market copies of different English-speaking bands' videos. All the time I wanted to learn more.

And then me and my friends started to learn from other sources, like from Western movies. We'd put black tape over the subtitles and keep listening to the whole movie and translate it, and if there was a commercial we'd discuss it between us like, "Okay, what did he just say?" For me, I had these simple notebooks and if I didn't know a word, I wrote it down and I'd keep asking.

I remember I watched *Air Wolf* a lot. Actually I think that was my nickname at the time. I love that movie. What else? I can't remember. *ET* maybe?

Man, I was into Western culture. I'm still into it. I love the American accents. I was really into cowboy movies, spaghetti Westerns. I'd like to go to Texas, have a ranch and a bunch of cattle and horses and ride all day. Hollywood movies taught me a lot: the accents, the language. I'm not saying I speak it fluently, but I took some part of it or I'm still trying to take it.

There's no kid in any part of the world that grew up in an established culture and found himself still in love with it when he was an adolescent. It's only after he grows up and faces the fact that this is the community he came from that he appreciates it. Now after all the things that I've done and have happened, leaving Iraq and stuff, it's only now I've started to listen to some Iraqi music. I keep crying sometimes because I miss that world. Maybe the culture reminds me of the old days, and I appreciate it more now.

But when you are fifteen, you are just like, "*Terminator* rules!" I was even into *Top Gun*. Yeah, in that movie Tom Cruise was a big shot, you've got to admit it.

FIRAS: When I first started listening to rock, I was pretty much into Metallica, Slayer, and Death. Before Death, I had records by a band I knew called Sabbath. It's like a death metal band, old school. I also listened to *Black* Sabbath, but Sabbath is a totally different band. And then, I listened to more bands and records, just expanding my knowledge, testing the music. I would get these records through people that I knew. We used to have a couple of places in town where you could find things; sometimes they were hidden behind the pop and stuff. Every once in a while, you'd go there and they'd show you all the new stuff. We also just read magazines like *Bass Player, Metal Hammer, Metal Maniacs,* and find out what was coming out. Sometimes our friends would make us copies of albums, too.

WALEED: I didn't quite like metal that much until I had an epiphany. One day I had a very bad headache. For a practical joke my friend gave me two pills used to treat schizophrenia and told me they were headache pills. So I took them and I got high as shit. And I also had a wedding to go to!

So at the wedding I'm totally high, and, oh God, it was so embarrassing and now I'm thinking, I cannot go home like this. My mother would kill me. My dad would put a bullet in me. So I went and drank shitloads of coffee and smoked shitloads of cigarettes. I must have smoked a whole pack or something and I was still high. For some reason, I ended up going to a music store and feeling that I really wanted to listen to some metal.

The guy in the shop had a really old Walkman cassette player and I told him to play me the harshest, most messed-up metal that he had. He was like, "Are you angry?"

"Yes!"

"Okay, then this should sort you out."

And he put on *Roots* by Sepultura. And I listened to it over and over and over that night.

I must have listened to it like seventeen times in a row. I was trying to make sense of what was going on in my head and my body. But then it all made sense, I needed to scream. And that's what I needed to know to be a metal singer.

FAISAL: The first Metallica album I heard was the *Black Album*, in 1991. I actually didn't have the record, I had the video. It was very simple videos of Metallica, and I really enjoyed "Sad but True" and "Nothing Else Matters." After that I bought the symphony concert video in 1999. I really loved that show, so I started to collect all the albums, and then the concerts. I would go back by years, getting *Master of Puppets, Kill 'Em All*, and I even gathered some old shitty movies just to see them when they were young. There was the video

Cliff 'Em All and I started to just see how they lived, where they got their influences, their experience, their lifestyle, who formed the band, and why and how they formed it. All these details. Like you're studying, you keep reading and knowing a lot of bands.

I thought that these bands, like Metallica and Slayer, were playing some cool guitar. We would buy pirate copies of their videos and their albums on the black market because the official releases were not available in Iraq. It was my brother, Naif, and his friends who first exposed me to metal. You have to understand that we grew up in a very simple community, a very simple society. Nobody actually cares about heavy metal, just about putting food on the table, being able to survive from day to day, and nothing else.

I started being friends with Marwan when he knew that I was into heavy metal. He said, "Well, man, that's cool, I listen to Metallica sometimes, some songs, but I never actually go into it that much," but we shared some ideas of getting a band together ourselves.

MARWAN: In my family there was a lot of tension and arguments that I witnessed and I hated everything about it, but I had to repress it and I couldn't really live my teenage years. We were growing up so fast, so it was the anger in metal music that I identified with. Plus, I could really relate to the lyrics. I remember literally banging my head against the wall with my friends to the song "Roots Bloody Roots" and when the song was finished I felt pacified. I crawled all over the floor, did some crazy, stupid stuff, stuff you'd only see in a mosh pit, but I felt refreshed. I wanted a bigger dose. What I was getting from regular music was not enough. Having that and feeling the changing phases of my life, I began to feel more responsible toward my environment that I was living in, my mum, my dad, my sisters, and there was no one there to support the family. I realized I couldn't live inside my head forever and that no one would step up and help you—you had to help yourself and your family. Plus, there

TONY, MARWAN, AND FAISAL AT THE PRACTICE SPACE, BAGHDAD, LATE 2003.

was a shortage of a lot of things like food and medical supplies in Iraq at the time, and the economy was really weak. My mom and dad were living the daily struggle. That was when I began to have my own lifestyle. I began to work out why I was not so acceptable to the community—I was just different from them, I talk about different things than them, what I wear is a little different from them, my goals are different from them, and that is why they couldn't communicate with me: They couldn't accept me the way I am, and at the time, I didn't really understand that I *was* different.

FAISAL: I've worn jeans my whole life, never traditional Arabic costume, but when I got into metal I started dressing more cooler, like slashing my pants a little. I got a lot of T-shirts, my first one was the . . . *And Justice for All* one. I've still got it; it's kind of been torn away. It's in my closet back in Baghdad, underneath everything. I loved that shirt. I bought it from a secondhand store in Baghdad called Balla. Sometimes kids kept selling their own shirts because you can't find new shirts, and even if you can find any, it's very expensive. Twenty bucks for a new shirt—that was huge money for me. So I couldn't afford it. Secondhand shirts for like five or six bucks was a very good price for me as a kid.

No one minded me dressing like that. I mean, it's a simple shirt, you used to be able to wear whatever. Sometimes I'd find some salesman in the street and they'd be selling potatoes or carrots or whatever and wearing some Slayer or Sepultura or Iron Maiden shirt, by accident—they just bought some shirt in the market. It's a very good thing, though, when you see it, you're like, "Oh my God," and sometimes we ask if they want to trade, even if it's smelly, I didn't care, as long as this band or that band was on it.

All that has changed now—since the U.S. invasion, it has become harder to dress freely. Now it's dangerous. After the occupation you could get killed for it. People would think you were devil worshipers or Americanized, and just because we are wearing that shirt or necklace or any kind of costume, it was like, "Earrings? Don't even think about it. Grow your hair long? Don't even think about it." Before the occupation, it was cooler.

MARWAN: Before I was into metal, most of the time I was hanging with kids and most of the kids are sitting around, eating sunflower seeds on the side of road, the power's off, it's hot and humid, we'll just walk around the block, talking about nothing but cars, or this guy or that guy or some fight that had happened; we didn't have much else, but every now and then we found fun or productive stuff do. I remember my friends and I went to a college nearby and we used to play basketball there in the evenings, and later I joined the team for like two years. Or we'd fly kites or shoot marbles. Some of them are good memories, of us just hanging out on the block. But things started to change around the time the band formed.

FIRAS: I started playing music around 1998. I played classical guitar for a while. Tony and I used to go to some teacher before Saad Zai. His basic knowledge was built on personal experience. Like, nobody taught him before or anything. So he used to play Arabic songs. I started learning, for three or four months, classical guitar lessons. And my obsession with the bass started in that time. I like music to be loud and kind of bass-heavy, like shaking the seat. And so I liked the sound of it. After that, through Tony, I also met Saad Zai.

The idea after we met him was to stick together and play and be better and better. The first time I met Saad, he was shredding the guitar in front of me and I just shut up and listened.

FAISAL: I wanted to start a band but I couldn't even afford one string on an instrument. So I started to look for work and found something with a commercial band for kids.

It was like a circus; they'd just started to do some fund-raising and parties for children, for Christians. You know, like simple parties. I went to a lot of them. I started working with this band a lot—they paid me like two and a half dollars a night, and I would, like, carry instruments for them and stuff.

You do whatever it takes, you know. They'd dress as clowns and jump around to please the kids, it was kind of like foreign music but they mixed it with Arabic music. After a while I came up with the idea that I wanted to sing. So I told them I wanted to sing with their band. I told them I could sing in English and they said, "Really? Can you copy some pop music?" and I was like, "Yeah, whatever." I sang Ace of Base.

It seems crazy now, but I would have done anything. They said, "Okay, we want you to do a bit of singing with some dancing parts now." I was like, "Errr, okay, dude." After that I started training the whole class how to move and dance. Seven guys, all dudes.

We would perform at a club called Hayla Hoop ["Hula Hoop" in Arabic] and I would make about ten thousand dinars, ten bucks. After that I bought a bass guitar. It was an old Aria Pro II. It was brown, a woody brown with one pickup. The paint was all smashed off so I had to polish it up and clean it up for the band. Actually I painted it a lot of colors, like blood red, then black, then brown again.

After a while I had to get an amplifier, so I started to play with the clown group again. You have to perform to get some money to buy an amplifier.

My parents were so proud because it was the motive for me [to start working]. I could have carried on studying, but I went to my father and I told him I wanted a bass guitar. He looked me up and down and said, "What?"

"Dad, I want a bass guitar."

"Faisal, what is a bass guitar?"

"It's like a guitar, but with a long neck and four strings."

"What are the strings?"

"Dad, it's a guitar, okay?"

"Well, you can't get a guitar."

"Why? Naif has a guitar."

"Naif has his own money, so if you want your own guitar you have to get your own money. I can't afford a bass guitar for you."

So then I realized he was saying, "Get a job, quit depending on me."

Then I found another job for a telephone company in my neighborhood, working on the reception, delivering phone calls to engineers and stuff. I was about seventeen. It helped me buy a bass amp because my salary was about thirty bucks a month. I was a temporary employee. I worked there for about six or seven months. It was a very little amp called an EX5. It had just one volume, one bass, and I couldn't turn up the whole levels. Playing it in the house, I was only allowed to get the volume up to 1. That was the limit—after that I'd get punished. I tried to learn "My Friend of Misery" by Metallica by playing along to it on the stereo. I had started to collect my own music, and I really loved playing solo on the bass guitar. Cliff Burton was the biggest influence on me. He was more than a bass player—he was really something. When I first started listening to Metallica, I didn't know he was dead. After my brother told me he died in '87, it was a very sad moment:

"He's dead? This is not Cliff Burton?"

"No, Faisal, this is Jason Newsted."

"Ohhh man, he sucks."

After a while I started to like Jason Newsted because the first time I listened to "Blackened," it crushed my bones. I was playing my bass guitar next to my little stereo. I rewound the song to the beginning and thought, Okay, it's going to be a long, long road for me and a lot of practice. In the end I kind of learned it. I still made a lot of mistakes on it, but at least I knew where I was supposed to go.

MARWAN: I'll tell you about Faisal. Faisal had a "symphony." We used to call it a symphony because there were so many people in it. It was people who had equipment, people who knew his brother, people who sold CDs and records, people who wanted to be musicians. They were all in it. He knew a lot of people connected to the underground music scene in Iraq. So one day Faisal and like twenty other guys announced they were doing a concert. Yes, twenty people in a band. It sounded weird to me when I heard about it. I'd never been to a live concert in my life, so it was a big deal for me. They were our friends, we wanted to support them, they were going to get some money out of the tickets, and we were going to go and have some fun. They invited a lot of people because when there's something happening with music in Baghdad, everybody knows about it because there's not much happening here music-wise and word spreads quickly through the underground music community. I called about nine or ten of my friends so they could come, as well. I figured the more, the better.

FAISAL: This was not Acrassicauda's first gig, this was still the Hello V.O.Y. band—it was the same group that we formed in the BIS. We were going to play different styles but most of it was like Bryan Adams stuff, and sometimes we tried to copy some boy band music and some Metallica songs. But I never had a chance to practice with the band—I just thought that gathering a lot of people together was a band. I never put in my mind that forming a band means a lot of practice, a lot of days. It doesn't happen suddenly. After that, things started getting better because I started to learn a lot.

MARWAN: So yeah, the "symphony" concert never came to be. They called us and they said, "Oh, the drummer broke his leg." But they didn't even have a drummer. It was just a lie and a big disappointment for me and the ten guys who were lining up at my house, ready to go wearing their T-shirts and chains. So I was like, "What about the people I called, what about the people who have already bought their tickets?" They had to go AWOL from the concert hall.

FAISAL: I ended up forming a band with six different guitar players, and I organized and sold tickets for a concert even though I didn't have a drummer. Only sixteen people bought the tickets. And I had to refund them all.

MARWAN: It was a total disappointment. And that was the end of the symphony. So we met up, me and Faisal, and he was talking about his passion for Metallica, and I was listening to stuff like Metallica and Scorpions, and we started hanging out together and he played a little bit of guitar, and every day there was like ten guys hanging out in his room. Everyone used to gather down there. His house was like a cafeteria: They were always offering us food and coffee. Faisal knows a lot of people, I'll give him that. So we met and talked about starting a band and me playing the drums. The thing is, in Iraq, we have like two or three drummers, that's it. In the whole of Iraq. So it's hard, you can't make a band with no drummer. Nobody wants to take that responsibility, playing drums, and where are you going to practice? How much can you afford to pay? So he tried to get me to form the band, maybe as a drummer. Before, in the fourth grade, I had already played percussion, bongos, through my dad. He already had them and he used to play them sometimes. My sister used to play the keyboard and accordion. She started in primary school, and it was my dad's keyboard—he loved to use the prerecorded beats and play one note at a time, for hours. So we had musical instruments before, and it was something that we did for fun, like at birthday parties and stuff. Then in the fourth grade I participated in a celebration, like a march, playing snare drum. So I told Faisal that, and he was like, "Yeah, cool, dude, so what about it?" and I was like, "I don't know, I always wanted to play guitar." But the idea of drums sounded tempting.

FAISAL: I started to hang out with Waleed and Marwan at the same time. Not together, but during the same period. I shared with Marwan a lot of ideas about forming a band, and with Waleed a lot of ideas about how we make music, and I tried out a lot of different people altogether.

MARWAN: Faisal would do things like meet somebody in the street and go, "Oh, you're a singer, join the band," and it was like, "Oh, here we go, another dozen people who can't sing for shit." So I believe when Faisal and I met, it made the project serious. When we started, I had to buy a drum kit. I remember he called me that day and said, "There's a guy I know who sells drums and musical equipment, maybe he can get you a drum kit."

I was like, "Dude, I can't afford a drum kit, I'm not working, I just told you about my circumstances." Deep down I wanted one, but financially, it was so far from happening.

But then, he tells me the name of the store and I'm like, "Hold on a minute, that sounds familiar."

So I called my dad, and I'm like, "What's my older cousin's name?" and he confirmed it, so I told Faisal, "Dude, this is my cousin you're talking about." I took Faisal and went to my cousin. He had the biggest store at that time, and he sold drums and also some antique equipment, like back to the dark ages of music. He sees me first, and we hadn't seen each other for ten years, and he's fifty-five years old. I told him, "I need a drum kit."

My dad had already said, "You can't afford that." But the family relationship helped get a deal, and plus he and my father had an old rivalry, so it was tempting for him to find a way to torture my dad. I got the drums from him, and I told him I'd pay like five thousand a month or something. I still haven't even finished paying him back. So it was thanks to him that I was able to get the drums. The minute I walked in with the twenty-two-inch bass drum, my dad tells me, "Get that thing out of the house. You're not going to sleep in the house tonight! What is this? Like a nightclub?" And I remember the two guys who helped me carry the drums scattered the minute they saw him come out. They knew my dad had a temper, and they didn't want to mess with that. My dad's kind of a scary guy, intimidating.

I left the drum kit for about three days in front of the house, in the garage, in protest. The third day, my dad told my sister to tell me to put them inside, because he and I weren't on speaking terms. I protested and refused to submit. My dad called my cousin and told him, "Why'd you sell him drums? We don't need any more of this in our lives." My cousin used to play bass for a while and they thought it was a disgrace for the family, because they associated it with nightclubs and stuff.

My cousin told him, "Don't worry about it, he can't put these drums together, they're falling apart." I heard that on the upstairs phone and it was like a challenge. Everything's a challenge for me. So I used my dad's tools, put the drums together without him knowing, and then I started practicing.

I told myself, Until you practice, there is nothing close to a band, so they can continue with their symphonies. But things weren't going the way Faisal and I planned. There are things that you know rationally and instinctively are right, and this is wrong. Having four singers in the band is wrong. Having one singer is right. Having six guitarists with no solo guitar who can't play for shit is wrong. Having two guitarists who can both play is right. So basically, Faisal and I started putting jam sessions together in my house. A lot of tea, cookies, chain-smoking, and a lot of crappy sounds. We went from playing covers of other bands to trying to come up with our own sound. We were into it, but we weren't ready yet.

FAISAL: We got our experience jamming together to see who was the best. I had a lot of friends who played guitar and I didn't even know who to choose. I got them in, many of them, one by one, to see who had the spirit to play in the way I wanted, and from all these friends I never found one. So I formed another band, Volcano, with a friend who could barely play but it never lasted. We organized a concert for twenty-two days in the future, but in the run-up we only produced one song. A guitarist named Waleed Khaled played okay, and we tried to talk to him about taking his music to the next level, but he didn't want to hear it. He wanted to be the lead guitarist but he couldn't play so well. So we had to take him out of the band. Actually Marwan did, because I never had the guts to kick one of my best friends out of the band.

WALEED RABIA: In 1999 we started a group called Volcano and I was asked to sing. I was like, "You're fucking kidding me, I can't sing for shit."

In my family, being an artist or a singer was something that was associated with alcoholism and nightclubs. It was something that would bring great shame upon them. But in the end I confronted my family about my singing. So we started another band named Phoenix and we would rehearse at a CD store. The band then was Marwan, myself, Hassan (who owned the store), Faisal, and a guy that we knew through Hassan named Minnar.

FAISAL: With Phoenix, I changed to guitar. Hassan the bass player had one of the CD stores we used to work at, and in the back of his house, there was a very long garage. We went in there and painted it and cleaned it because he'd been keeping his dog in there. After that we brought in Marwan's drums, and I brought my guitars and the little amplifier. We started jamming for a little while, but even that didn't work, because we worked in the store, as well, and the hours of store work started going down, so the bass player and guitar player didn't show up every day, so there was me and Marwan and Waleed left, and we had to cross over from a distance to get there. Marwan and Waleed both came from a different direction, right straight into my neighborhood, so it was a long walk just to be in the band and to go to work. It didn't seem so fair for us. So the guys said, "If we're going to get a good start, we have to clean up our act musically."

We had no role models in Iraq, no one to give us advice about how to start our own band. So we started looking for someone to teach us. At that time we became more experienced, and then we found a man called Saad Zai. He was so generous, so kind. He was older than us,

BACK ROW: FIRAS, TONY, FAISAL, AND FRIEND; WALEED IN FRONT. TONY IS HOLDING A
FLYER FOR THE THIRD GIG IN BAGHDAD, WHICH WAS RIGHT BEFORE THE WAR, 2003.

so much wiser and more experienced, but when you talked to him, it was just like he was the same age and had our same way of thinking. He was so inspiring to all of us.

TONY: Firas was the first person I met in the band. We studied together under Saad Zai's supervision. I am not sure what attracted me to metal—maybe the circumstances we lived in drove us to listen to heavy metal music. It affected us in such a strong way that we liked this kind of music better than any other. Also, Saad was into metal himself and that's what we liked about him, plus he was a distinguished musician. He would give us ideas and thoughts, and he would tell us what it would be like if we ever really formed a band. He would tell us what kind of equipment to get, what sounded right and what didn't musically. He always had bad luck concerning bands, but he was still enthusiastic, and encouraged us to start one. I believe he's one of the most dedicated musicians I got to meet through this musical journey. We've been very fortunate to have him on our side.

FIRAS: The guys went to Saad Zai because they wanted a guitarist, and he referred them to Tony. He said, "I have this student who is good. He's also thinking about making a band." After that, Tony came and talked to me about it. We didn't really have a band together, but we liked to jam with each other. He said, "Okay, I've got these guys that want to set up a band, so I probably won't be able to play with you," and stuff like that.

I suggested the idea that I go play with Marwan a little, not to be in the band or anything, but just to practice. So I hung out with him for a couple of days and started practicing with him. I thought, Sure, why not formally join the band? It was also practice for me and for my skills, and it was fun, 'cause music's what I wanted to do. Not necessarily being in a band, but music. And the band was a good opportunity to play even more music, and play as a group. That was the part that was missing from my musical experience. I got to the point where I had to be more creative and challenge myself, try to be the best for the band. Do hard work just to benefit the band in the end.

We never thought about the style—it just happened to be metal. For me and Tony it was always about rock and metal, because that's what we were used to. The first riffs that I started to learn on bass were Metallica and Overkill bass lines.

Saad Zai taught all of us, one way or another, and gave us instructions, gave us advice, stuff that we needed, and gave us the motive and the attraction to the music. He helped us build the band by giving us the structure we needed. The best advice he gave us was "Practice, practice, practice." That's the main thing, and the other thing is "Don't let anybody in the band pull you down. If you want to keep them in the band, you have to pull them up. If you can't pull them up, just get rid of them." Saad Zai is up north now. He's a refugee in his own country. He's a session player these days: He plays for other groups, not really rock, just regular pop songs or whatever.

FAISAL: Saad gave us a motive to play well. He made you understand all of your mistakes so that you could do the right thing in the future. I took about nine or ten classes from him but I couldn't handle the practicing. He always said I was bad at that. And then Marwan had two or three practices drumming. When we would practice downstairs, he'd hear one wrong note and come down to correct us. And then I started to go in and ask Saad, "Please teach us something to start with. We want to form a band but we don't know anything. Just teach us the basic rules." And he was so kind and generous about it. He started teaching us, leading us in the right way, in the direction that we needed. He told us every single detail that we should do and not do and eventually, with him to help us, we started to make it happen. We would spend the whole time practicing. Six, nine, twelve hours at a time.

MARWAN: When we met Tony, we were told he had skills because he was studying with Saad. For me, I was welcoming any kind of SOS solutions at that point. Saad was like a father figure to Acrassicauda. His store was close by, in the same building where we practiced, but at the beginning he didn't like us at all. Everything about us was messy: We didn't have the right formation for the band, we didn't have any amplifiers or the right equipment, we weren't organized, and there was no sound for the band or plans set ahead about producing music. But when Tony came, he had a big hundred-watt amp. He came and had the right tune for a distorted guitar. It was like, "This guy is on the right track!" which I guess was thanks to Saad.

I was like, "Okay, that's how we're starting." Waleed Khaled, the guitarist, and Tony didn't get along. Actually Waleed didn't get along with anyone, musically. His whole idea of music was not formed yet and his influences were probably different. So, two months later, Tony left the band.

He was like, "I can't work like this." But we had also got to meet Firas in that time. Tony had brought Firas to the band and Tony had said, "This is my friend, I can't play without him." So I played with Firas, we jammed with him, and this was their first time playing with live drums. They loved it. We kind of clicked, not right away but we were just starting. So that left Firas . . . Tony . . . Faisal was the bassist as well, so two bassists now . . . two guitarists . . . one drummer . . . and one singer. But I guess that's just my opinion. You see bands like Slipknot with nine members in it, or black metal bands with six members in them, and everybody's doing their part. But the way that we were doing it was just not organized enough. So that's what happened. Tony left the band because he didn't get on with Waleed Khaled. And now Faisal was just sitting around in the practice space doing nothing because Firas was playing bass.

Faisal says, "You know what? Maybe I should quit, too." So what happens is, I start arguing a lot with Waleed Khaled and I'm having a lot of problems with him so I don't show up to practice because I don't want to jam with him. It wasn't personal, but it was draining because of all the arguments. Then we make a decision that Waleed should go. He's not producing anything, but he's my friend, as well as a cool, funny guy. But on the musical level we don't click, or with the guys as well. So we agreed that the three of us should talk to him, but at the last minute they all abandoned me and I had to face him alone. So I go down there. I'm sitting in the practice space, he comes in, I close the door, and I tell him, "I don't think we should work together on the

THE BAND WITH OTHER STUDENTS OF SAAD ZAI'S
AT THE PRACTICE SPACE IN BAGHDAD, CIRCA 2005.

music anymore." He smashes stuff, he takes his guitar, curses at me, and gives me the middle finger, and he goes away.

I felt really bad at first, but if it was right for the band, I'll do it, even if it means losing a good friend. So I believe at that time, Faisal watched Waleed walk away and that made him really upset. He said, "Why did you do that?" I was already in a bad mood because I had to let my friend go. I guess it's always been Faisal who hires the members, and me who fires them.

So I told him, "You know what? That's it, it's the day of crucial decisions. We have to get this band on its feet." I called Tony, asking him to come back, and Faisal went to get him. So they came back a few hours later with the amplifier, and we told him Waleed was gone. So now it's me, Tony, Faisal as a guitarist, Firas as a bassist, and Waleed Rabia as a singer. That's who's left. And we called for a practice. And that was the birth of Acrassicauda.

The first time we all played together, it felt so right and the foundations were set. Everybody knew what to do, there was no confusion, and apart from everything that happened that day, I believe the minute we all walked out of the practice space, there was no remorse.

WALEED RABIA: At first I had my reservations about the band because I was intimidated. They were all excellent musicians and all I could do was scream. Looking at Tony play the guitar was amazing. His fingers were like water running down a creek. Looking at Faisal coming with new ideas was mind-blowing. And Marwan with his energy, like a driving force. And Firas's bass lines were just awesome.

One of the first times we got together, the five of us, with Firas and Tony, as well, we played "Turn the Page" by Metallica. Tony was like, "I like your voice. We can do something together." Tony is the sweetest, most respectful person you can meet. Firas is awesome and funny as hell.

MARWAN: I remember one day after school I came to the practice space and saw Firas playing. He didn't even lift his eyes from the bass. I still remember that. It was only when he saw me sit behind the drums that he looked up with his big smile. After that he told me that it was the first time that he had played with live drums. I remember we talked about tempo and he just thought it was great to be playing with the band and then we just began to get along. There was no effort to make friendship with any one person more than the others—we all just got along really well, even if sometimes there was tension. We just dealt with it, 'cause after all, what's good for the band comes first, not necessarily the individuals in it.

Firas was doing that slap bass and we made a song called "The Doll" with it. He was bringing songs to the band, I was putting words to them, and me and him just got on. We actually did a solo together at one of our concerts, just the two of us.

FAISAL: The first practice of the full band that would eventually become Acrassicauda was in summer 2001. And we had a concert organized for twenty days after that.

MARWAN: The problem was Waleed Khaled had booked a concert for us—he went and agreed with the people on the concert. A concert that we didn't have songs for, in only twenty days. We couldn't cancel because we didn't want people to think it was another "symphony." That day, we produced three songs. We came up with "Psycho," "Since You're Gone," and "Massacre." That's it, we clicked, everybody knew that it was right. So we started practicing and we were ready by the time of the concert. We were practicing for ten or twelve hours straight every day to make the deadline. And it was a very productive period, especially with the help of Saad. We didn't even want to sleep or eat so we could keep practicing. Everyone had a pile of ideas that we just wanted to get right and share. Now we had something others didn't have—the band.

Sometimes we had, like, a nervous breakdown. I remember Firas going out, shouting like a crazy person one time. I went out after him and he was pacing up and down, saying something like, "I can't take it, I can't take it," because the intensity of the music and the long hours we were doing were getting to him. It was hard fucking work, every day, ten to twelve hours a day. But it was also the first time that we felt it was a band. It was not bullshit. We were too proud and too enthusiastic to admit that it was hard for us to do that much work. Now, looking back on it eight years later, it was totally worth it.

AcrassicaudA

Live Concert

Part (1).

- 1- The Final countdown   (**Europe**)
- 2-   45   (**Shinedown**)
- 3- Out side   (**Staind**)
- 4- Here Without you   (**3 Three Doors down**)
- 5- Knock on Heaven's Door   (**Gun'n Roses**)
- 6- Fade to Black   (**Metallica**)
- 7- Holiday   (**Scorpions**)

Part (2).

- 1- One   (**Metallica**)
- 2- Bother   (**Stone sour**)
- 3- Loser   (**3 Doors Down**)
- 4- Numb   (**Linkin Park**)
- 5- Behind Blue Eye's   (**Limp Bizkit**)
- 6- Nothing Elss Matter   (**Metallica**)
- 7- When the Angel Fall's   (**ACRASSICAUDA**)

- Regret....

Anathema

Pink Floyd

LIVE UNDEAD

FAISAL: Our first concert was kind of crazy. It was at an art gallery called the Aurfally Club. It was kind of the only place where new bands could play. There were piano classes in the back and a very big garden and an open gallery inside it. We used to hold the concerts in the garden. We had two there and a lot of people went to them. Half of them were our friends and families, and the other half were people that we didn't know. Most of them were young men, and some were old musicians. Some guys were in their late thirties and really into metal. Most of the other bands who played there were either session musicians or into classical music. We were the only band left who still played this kind of music at that time.

We were called Acrassicauda for that first concert.

MARWAN: When we first started the band, we were concentrating more on getting everything right musically, and didn't think about the name. But we would always see these black scorpions in the practice space, and we found out they were this kind of scorpion that only lives in the Iraqi desert—its Latin name is *acrassicauda*. We could relate to this as a name in many ways. Plus, we liked the idea of it being in an ancient language; it was something eccentric.

WALEED: The first two times we played were at the Aurfally gallery. The third was at the Rebat Hall, which was the ultimate for us.

At the first show, I was so scared. I was about to shit my pants. It was such an intimidating feeling.

I remember setting up and we were exchanging these glances, like it was a big deal, and it was.

We were expecting about fifty fans but in the end we got more than four hundred people. This added to the nervousness—I was like, "I'm about to break now."

Marwan said, "Shut up, we're going to finish when we finish."

MARWAN: For the first concert, we had to rent equipment. I went to my cousin's store and we rented hundred-watt amps and stuff. We knew we had to bring it live. We had songs of our own and we had five covers, including David Bowie's "The Man Who Sold the World," "Nothing Else Matters" by Metallica, and "Patience" by Guns N' Roses. Mostly it was ballads or just plain rock music. We tried to go nice and easy on the audience. Little did we know that our friends and audience were hardcore—they weren't joking at all. Mostly they demanded the real deal, stuff like Slayer and early Metallica.

Two hundred and fifty to three hundred people showed up, and right away they demanded another concert. After a month we did a second show. The third concert was at the Rebat Hall, which is a big, big symphony hall. We were shocked about that. I remember during the first song . . . we played the intro, we had a name now and some fans, and I remember breaking two sticks in the first song because I was so excited I was hitting the drums really, really hard. Four hundred people showed up to that concert. They were headbanging and shouting the band name. That was massive. I'll remember that forever. There were also tiny bits of blood here and there. I know we should feel bad about it, but it was fun. We loved it as the band was arranging more stuff, producing more music, and standing on more solid ground. But we didn't determine a style, because we had a lot of variety. We'd go from alternative to like doom and death metal stuff, and we'd go into singing pop rock, so it was like that. It was a lot of pressure because we wanted to determine a style, but we couldn't do that yet—we were getting a varied audience because of the different tastes that people had at the time. After a while we stopped worrying about it.

FAISAL: I was nervous before that first show. I was scared, but I felt some strange kind of confidence in myself, too. Maybe because of the unorganized groups I had formed before, I had that super-energy in my body. I thought to myself that I should do something, and if I'm not going to prove myself in this concert, then I'll quit. I believed that forty-five percent of me was nervous to death and fifty-five percent was so confident you couldn't even imagine, and after a couple of songs, I started headbanging even though the people were just sitting down watching.

Waleed was singing. There were three or four cover songs. We always do different ones every concert—it's like a tradition for the audience, just to satisfy them. We also played "Youth of Iraq."

WALEED: "Youth of Iraq" was a tribute to Saddam. We wrote it the day before the concert. It was the fastest-created song in history. I wrote the lyrics in two and a half minutes and they wrote the music in fifteen.

FIRST CONCERT
AFTER THE
WAR, HINDYA
CLUB, BAGHDAD,
2004.

And, lyrically, it was something we were not proud of at all. But we had to write a song for the regime, and the regime was very much against Israel. We were raised on images of Palestinians being tortured.

Saad Zai told me to write it. And it was because of the story of a guy called Berge, who started this Iraqi heavy metal band called Scarecrow.

Berge had long hair and a goatee beard. He ended up having his head shaved by the Secret Service and beaten up onstage while he was performing because they said he was doing "Satanic verses."

MARWAN: "Youth of Iraq"? We can't get that monkey off our backs—no one can let that one go. Saad came to us and told us that when he had his band Passage, he wrote a song for Saddam because if you do that, then the police will leave you alone. We had told him that we were feeling a little intimidated because we were singing in English, but Saad said that we should do that song. He was looking out for us. Then I guess Waleed came back with "Youth of Iraq." Saad gave us the riff. We used to call it the "blanket song." It covered our asses. Luckily, nothing happened to us.

FAISAL: We had to do "Youth of Iraq" because we got told about people looking at our lyrics and saying we were trying to speak against the government, but none of this happened. As much as we tried to take this band to success, we had to not take our chances and obey all the rules.

It was really kind of scary just to think about it, the idea of government restriction. The first concert, we didn't even notice but there were hundreds of people sitting in the garden, watching your moves, watching what you're going to sing. We couldn't tell if one of these guys was a secret agent, pretending to be one of the audience and waiting for the right moment to come. We were so careful not to mention anything specific to nail us. It didn't happen and we were so glad about it, but also we were sad because nobody was cheering—you felt like art was not that powerful in our country. But the good thing in Iraq is that whenever there is an awesome band or a new band is playing, everyone starts gathering around to see who it is.

At the first show, a lot of friends showed up, and we felt like we kind of proved something. We maybe made a couple of friends upset because of the financial thing—we didn't get a strong financial return from the tickets. But we were so happy because a lot of people started talking about us and saying it was a good show and giving us their comments and stuff. My brother was so proud of me. I'd finally gone onstage and performed with my own band. It was a really kick-ass step for me.

There were some heavy-ish bands that came before us—I remember Scarecrow, Passage, Agony, and one called Converse. There were different kinds of styles: One band used to cover the Bee Gees, some were specifically Pink Floyd, and some covered Black Sabbath. There were other bands that were creating and producing their own songs, as well as doing covers, but they never lasted. I don't know what happened to them; they just disappeared. The only member left of Passage is Saad Zai. My brother went to their concert and he said they were really kick-ass. They played glam rock.

Nothing would happen to you if you dressed like a glam rocker, but you'd feel the eyes watching you when you walked; you just couldn't fit in. Iraq is a place where you can't imagine yourself wearing this kind of stuff. For me, I had long hair when I was into pop music—it wasn't longer than my shoulders, and perhaps just to my jaw, but whenever I walked around I felt like people believed I was gay. Like, "Who's that stupid homosexual?" I even had a couple of fights over it.

FIRAS: I would consider Iraqi metal fans to be the most hardcore dudes on this planet. Because they fucking risk and sacrifice their life just to get to a show. They risk being arrested or killed or bombed or *anything*, and they still attend the shows. And that's something really big. We really appreciate it, because it meant a lot to us—they were really supportive, and they don't just support metal but support *us*, you know? And that was a great feeling. I don't have the words for it.

FAISAL: People are sometimes caught up in waves of ignorance and they become blind and won't accept any kind of change to you or the people around you. This is the stupid thing that happens—maybe they weren't into that Western thing and they thought it shouldn't be so accepted into our community. I don't blame them; they were just raised in a very traditional society. If I was them I wouldn't pick a fight or be a bully. But I chose my way, and people should learn to mind their own business. I can't blame them because people change and I keep thinking that they'll change tomorrow and find someone who will change them. I wasn't an aggressive person—I was peaceful and most of the time I minded my own business.

FIRAS: The concert where we played in the symphony orchestra's venue, that was the last one before the 2003 war. We knew the war was coming because all the international media covered it. Like American newspapers, but European newspapers and magazines were full of it. Big names, you name it. They came to us and did an interview while we were practicing before the show. We pretty much had an agreement with the manager, to practice there for a while, so we had a week of that, and that was a really great show. I would consider it as my favorite so far. I'd never seen a crowd like that have the same dedication. There was a fair amount of girls there for the first time.

LAST CONCERT BEFORE THE WAR, RABBAT HALL, BAGHDAD, JANUARY 2003.

FAISAL: We didn't care about the money; whenever there was a financial issue we didn't care about it because we didn't have anyone dealing with that side of things. I don't remember that we had good financial gains from our concerts; we even paid for some ourselves out of our own pockets. We didn't care how long practicing took or how much expenses it took each day. I remember that Marwan and me, we used to finish school and go to the rehearsing place and sometimes we'd leave the house at ten or eleven and go to practice, then go to school and maybe back to practice. It was just something that we had to do.

It was the show at the symphony hall that stood out the most. The hall was built for the Iraqi Symphony Orchestra. We rented it, had to pay like twenty dollars, and we called it a "youth event" because we had to sign some papers for the Ministry of Culture to rent a hall like that.

Live Concert

**For all the rock fans
AcrassicaudA
A inviting you to have a special night
of pure
(ROCK) music
Held at the vitality café
Thursday The 14th/ December/
2006
So be there and have fun…………..
For any Information's you can contact
the Number of the Café
Tel: 562 9664 – 562 9663
Jaramana – Main Street – 50 m ahead of
Syriatel Services Center**

Back then, Tony was still in the army. It was about forty days before the war started. Tony had a broken arm—he had been in a mini-bus accident—so he spent the whole concert sitting down. Since then, that hall has been renovated. I saw the orchestra there and peace movements there, they all performed after us. Bands from Kuala Lumpur, Sweden, and everywhere came and played a concert for peace.

TONY: I almost couldn't play in the symphony hall show. I had broken my clavicle in a mini-bus accident, although I kept showing up to practice. At that time, I was still in the military, so sometimes I would show up to practice still in uniform. It was so weird to hold a guitar while still wearing those clothes. Because I was hurt, I couldn't hold the guitar so I had to sit all the time, even when we played the show.

FIRAS: There was kind of a peace movement going on, and they used to hold their shows in the same place. They had bands from Spain and Italy and all European countries there—they came and played their shows and supported the Iraqi people, voicing their opposition to the war.

None of the others were metal groups; they were like folk and traditional music, not big names. I mean, they might be big in their own countries, but we don't know them. So they were like showing off, playing there.

FAISAL: It was a kick-ass concert. There were hundreds of people. You just felt the stage moving and vibrating beneath your feet, giving you that energy, just like a heartbeat, like a pulse. We were playing as the clock was ticking down to the war, and there were a lot of demonstrations and a lot of protests. Many people don't realize that there were demonstrations here. It worked both ways. When the Americans showed up, we'd never seen a satellite dish or a cellphone or different news from local TV news or whatever, so they showed us these pictures from all around the world with all these people protesting over going to war with Iraq. We saw the whole street full of people waving their signs.

FIRAS: We felt okay at the end of the concert, although everybody knew what was coming. We had been through it before, in '91, the Gulf War. Nothing could be worse than '91, so we just were cool with it. We lived our life and did the show. It didn't mean a lot to us. I mean, the war is coming, so what? Because we lived through war all the time, it was nothing new; it's not like I've never seen a bombing before, or seen airplanes getting shot down, or seen somebody getting killed before. I had seen all that. A couple of months after that show, the war started.

FAISAL: Nobody actually believed that America and Britain were going to go to war with Iraq—they thought there was no chance they would try to force out a regime if you had to sacrifice a whole country. As youths, we never cared that much about politics.

It was presented abroad that we were living in fear, or under terror, but I never saw anything happening to my family once. I was never even stopped by a policeman to show my ID. I had to be able to prove I was a student so that I didn't have to go in the army, but I've never been insulted, never been accused, never been in a police station in my whole life and neither has my family, but there are all these rumors and sayings and stuff. One of them you'd hear is "People have nothing to do except complain." I mean, let's say you're living under a regime, any regime, and it's forcing you to do something, but it's giving you another option—it's giving you peace and security twenty-four/seven, maybe not the best salaries you can imagine but at least you can put some food on the table. People still want to mind their own business, they want to serve their country,

THE BAND'S FIRST-EVER SHOW, AURFALLY CLUB, BAGHDAD, 2001.

and they want to be left alone. The regime might have been through a lot of war, a lot of people might have been separated and I don't know why, but I can't say a bad word about a president who made me live well in Baghdad. I can't just ignore him and say he wasn't part of my life. I grew up under his rules, and so did my family.

We didn't believe that anyone could do such a thing as invade us. Maybe, because there was a huge peace movement at the time, we thought, They wouldn't do that, they'll change. Eventually they all changed their minds. All I can remember is life was going normally and nobody was feeling that there'd be a war tomorrow or whatever. People were saying, "There's gonna be no war, dude. There won't be a war. Don't worry about it."

VIEW OF AREA
OF SADDAM HUSSEIN'S
PALACE, NOW THE
INTERNATIONAL ZONE,
BAGHDAD, DECEMBER
2005. PHOTO BY
STUART GRIFFITHS.

5

ᑫEᒪᒪ
ᐱWᐱIᒣᐱ

FAISAL: In the run-up to the invasion, I would stay up late listening to the radio to see what was going on. They used to call me Batman. I was like a night person. One night I heard one of the stations saying, "There is only twenty-four hours left for Saddam Hussein to leave the government," and I was like, "What? Who can ever make such a decision like that?"

Then it changed. It got down to, "Now it's the last fifteen minutes for Saddam Hussein to give it up," and all I can think about is that it's like I'm watching a movie or something. They said that troops would start going in at the end of the fifteen minutes. Troops were already on the border, but nobody could believe it. People were like, "What? The Americans are going to come here? Nah, don't be silly about it." Then we started hearing all these sirens, things started getting messy, mosques started calling to prayer. Next we heard ambulance sirens heading to the highway, because my house was near it. You could hear the sound of the sirens gathering and then shooting and bombs rising one by one. I couldn't even see; I was downstairs and all the doors and windows were closed. You just cool it down for a little while, and nobody knows what's going to happen. Sometimes it would keep going on for a couple of days, and sometimes it would go for half an hour then stop for an hour. You didn't know which place they were fighting in or anything.

WALEED: On the first night of "shock and awe," I remember saying good-bye to some journalists I was working with (I was a translator and fixer for news agencies at the time). All the journalists were staying at the Fanar Hotel and I wanted to say good-bye for the last time because, quite honestly, we felt like, "That's it." And that night, before the bombings, everything was still, man, there was not a single person on the street apart from me. And then the bombing started.

The news people say it started on March 20, but it actually started the night before. I remember feeling that it was quite probable and almost inevitable that I was about to meet my destiny. Hearing about the preparations for this war we knew it would not be like anything that happened before. It would not be like Iran-Iraq, 1980, or the Gulf War. We knew it was going to be different.

You're helpless and you can't do anything about it. The best thing to do is to sit tight.

I took my family from my home to my mother's parents' house. It was very close to the action. The bombs were falling like rain everywhere. It was nonstop, nonstop, hearing one after another. I counted up until one hundred and then I lost count.

I went outside the next morning. I was riding my young cousin's bicycle and the sky was absolutely black due to the fact that Saddam had ordered the army to build big trenches around the city, fill them with pure crude oil, and burn them, so the city was engulfed in this massive black cloud. I thought to myself, If Werner Herzog were here to see this, he would think it was the best movie set ever.

It kind of looked like hell. And looking around me at the time, that's when I started questioning this thing about "smart bombs" and "We're using very sophisticated weapons," because it didn't look like that at all. They were saying they can target very specific things but these bombs were just going all over the place.

For example, the two-year-old child who was killed by this one bomb was not in Saddam's Secret Service.

MARWAN: I was at home when it happened. I didn't expect it. It was the planes and the helicopters and fighters in the sky. Plus the sirens. It gives me a feeling in my stomach every time I think about it. The air was heavy; at certain moments, like for three days after the war, it smelled like dead bodies, rotting bodies. It would bring the fragrance of death. You'd see people getting their shovels from their houses and burying the dead, whether they knew the people or not. One of my musician friends participated in burying anonymous people. Every time a breeze would come, it would bring the smell of death.

All the houses still had tape over the windows from the Gulf War. People never bothered to take it down.

Bombs started getting stronger and stronger. When it came to the morning it was a relief, you could actually get some sleep because the bombing would subside. It lasted for about forty days. I didn't give it much thought. I had to be strong in front of my family, seeing them shaking because they were all nervous.

I slept after it stopped and I woke up at eight, and my dad was awake. He left the house and his hair was even grayer. I don't remember seeing my dad like that before. It took twenty years from him, in five or six hours.

AMERICAN BLACK HAWK HELICOPTER PHOTOGRAPHED BY THE TIGRIS RIVER,
BAGHDAD INTERNATIONAL ZONE. PHOTO BY STUART GRIFFITHS.

The sounds coming from the invasion were like somebody trying to drive you insane, like a simulated hell on earth. You were in a room, and you heard people screaming like they're chopping people up. You heard running down the street, then you heard a grenade go off, like the war is in your backyard. You heard helicopters coming close, and the B-52 planes coming right near your house. You heard the massive engines like bees swarming, and you heard the hissing of the missiles.

They tell you to count like five seconds and you see where it impacts, so those five seconds determine your life. Every missile we heard was like the final fight. I remember the night that I was lying on the floor and I heard the missiles and just four shakes right underneath my hands and legs—I recall all this stuff. Waking up in the morning and going up to the roof to get the shreds of the bombs and the missiles, because you found them in your house. I had to sweep up pieces of metal, throw them in the garbage.

In '91, I saw these images. I was grown up enough to recognize the sound of the sirens and when it came back again, I had the same ache in my stomach. It was sheer madness. I didn't memorize it, but my stomach did. I remember the sounds they started using in the final days—to terrify people, these bombs that made sounds. It's like a psychological thing.

FIRAS: I was in my room sleeping when I was awoken by the explosions on the first day. It was like a rocket barrage. The first couple of days they would just, like, shoot rockets, hitting government buildings and stuff like that. For me it wasn't comparable to '91—'91 was the fucking worst shit. I'm talking about in a bombing way, not in terms of the overall result.

I was in my apartment. I mean, we have a basement under the building where everybody goes and uses it as shelter, but because we're used to it, we don't care about it anymore so we just sleep in our beds. Fuck it.

I didn't see much the next morning, but it started late at night and it continued until early morning, so they have this alarm going and they have this, not the release alarm, but like when everything stops they give you another alarm to tell you to go home or do whatever you want, just go back to your life. I remember one day I was standing on my balcony, stretching, waking up in the morning, and I looked up in the sky and I saw a fucking big ball of flame coming toward me. I didn't even think about it. Just, I'm dead. That's all I thought.

But that thing just flew by. I didn't know what the hell it was, and after half a second or so I heard the fucking blast, the boom, the explosion. I don't know, it was kind of a rocket or a bomb, I don't know what the hell it was but it scared me, it scared the shit out of me. After that, what worse could happen?

UNNAMED MILITIA IN ARMED CONFLICT IN BAGHDAD. PHOTO FROM EYEVINE.

TONY: When "shock and awe" started I was in the military camp—it wasn't an active duty camp, not a combat camp, more like writing books, signatures, and stuff. We didn't have to carry a rifle and go fight.

I was outside Baghdad, on the edges, the suburbs. It was at the top of hills so I could see the whole city. I saw the impact of the bombings on Baghdad. It was like I expected I was going to die, and at the same time I was thinking of my family, because it was dangerous down there. I was confused.

FAISAL: There were bullets flying all over the place. I remember going to my room to get something and hearing the bullets coming down on my roof. They were coming from the air. My family started to gather in the hallway away from the glass windows but I stayed in my room. I couldn't breathe so I just grabbed my pillow and went and slept in the living room. My mother kept screaming all night, "Faisal, come here, come back!" and I said, "Okay, when the shooting is done I'll come back." The living room wasn't a safe place to stay but I didn't want to hide.

On the first night I didn't get any sleep, but in the morning I was shocked to see what had happened. You don't believe it. You just think, What is this? How long is it going to take? Is it going to take another eight years like Iran? Is it going to last forever? We could die. It kept going on and on and on . . . It never stopped. It just kept falling down. You never knew whether it was going to hit your house or fall over you. You don't know, you just put yourself inside a box and never leave it, and no matter how strong your house is, upon which foundation it has been built, if one of these bombs hits your roof, then you're finished. There was a rocket that hit behind the mosque that our house was near to, about half a mile away. It was one of the biggest mosques Saddam built. This happened after about eight or nine nights of bombing. We left the house, we had to, because the whole street had locked their doors and left their houses. My brother and I wanted to stay at home but my parents said, "Let's go to your grandparents' house because staying here wouldn't be any use. We don't care if anyone is going to steal our stuff during this time. So let's stay at your grandparents' the whole night and see if it's better when we get back."

We had to see what kind of damages there were. There wasn't any, but there was a missile defender at the end of our street that the Iraqi army was at, and some of the soldiers had been killed.

We drove to my grandparents' house and it was still foggy and the city was full of Iraqi soldiers. Nothing had been occupied yet. It was from a storm of sand, pure red sand, not a yellow one or an orange one . . . I don't know why, it was really strange, it kept covering the whole city. It was like "blood day" or something. Kind of creepy. When you went out it was so hot and you were sweating and the sand was hitting your face. You could feel the dust on your tongue and inside your mouth. Our destination was near, just a couple of highways we had to cross to reach the other house.

I saw a lot of abandoned cars. New cars with their keys still in the ignition and doors open, because there was no gasoline. I also saw a lot of dead bodies, a lot of soldiers. There was a big hole full of dead bodies, one on top of the other, and nobody was paying any attention to them.

There were these soldiers with black uniforms. These were the jihad movement, which were the special forces, and there was the white uniform, who were the suicide squadron. These guys wear their own shroud on their skin so it's like they're ready to lose their life for their country. They are part of the army, but a special one, not like public guards. They're like deadly ones—you don't want to get near them. There were the dead at the side of the road, as well. These were horrible sights. Tragic. You don't want to live to see such days.

Things were so sensitive back then. No one knew what to expect when the American army landed. It didn't make any sense. We couldn't believe the first time we saw the Americans on our street, coming in and going around and checking out the whole neighborhood. There were tears in our eyes because it was almost like every single thing in our lives had vanished somehow. This was about twenty or twenty-one days after the cities in the south had been occupied. The Iraqi army started pulling back. All of them had thrown away their weapons and thrown off their uniforms so as not to be recognized. They'd just knock on the neighborhood doors and change their clothes. They got the orders that everything had fallen so they didn't have to fight anymore, and if you get these orders you're putting yourself in danger by staying in your uniform. The official line was: "You've got to save your own ass."

It's bad, but you try to convince yourself that maybe it's better for the country. Whatever kind of crime these soldiers committed to deserve to die like this, they were still defending the country they were born in. It's hard to imagine, but you can still remember it like it was yesterday. I still have my family living in the same fucked-up situation. There's no SOS call, no one to call in emergencies, there's nobody that can protect your rights that you already lost anyway. Sometimes you feel like the apocalypse is near, it's just a fucking dead end. There's no escape, there's no limit for it. You can't do anything.

I saw people stealing cars and looting stuff, and all I could hear was my parents saying, "Look what we've become. God have mercy on our souls." This was five years ago and every day you heard on the news about how many are injured and about how many car bombs went off. Well, they said the war would be finished in twenty-one days, but the war, and all the stuff that comes along with it, is still going on now.

The good thing was that I picked up my guitar. I couldn't leave it. It was a Gibson copy. I kept playing it underneath the sound of the bombs.

We stayed at my grandparents' home for fourteen or fifteen days. We had water until three days before the occupation, then they cut it off. For food, we had supplies from the government. Each person had the right to take supplies, so before the war they gave supplies for each person, enough for a whole year, so we didn't have much trouble. There were some main government offices where you would go to get them. After the war started, they were open one or two days. There were beans and rice. We had to buy some gas supplies for the war, about six cans they allowed for each house. But it didn't seem fair because sooner or later, these supplies were going to run out. Things started to quiet down, they started saying that the war was finished. The intense period lasted around twenty days and then the troops came in and started walking all over the streets. The twenty days were like the black days. No electricity. Red dust. You don't know whether you're going to live or die. I left the house to see a couple of friends a block away and as soon as I heard the sirens I ran back. It was so fucked.

FIRAS: A lot of people moved across town because in '91 some didn't, and they got hurt real bad. They thought this would be just like '91, so a lot of people did move out of Baghdad, to avoid losses. They might lose their house but they don't want to lose their lives, because '91 was just a whole fucking big mess. But I stayed at home.

I practiced, listened to records, and smoked cigarettes. That's all I did. The whole way we had until the last week or couple of days, before the taking over of Baghdad.

I got my brother woken up, and it was a fucking long day. In the morning there was a big fight in the palace, the presidential palace. A big fight, you couldn't see anything for the dirt. What I used to do, I just used to go up, it's like a seven-floor building, it's really high . . . I would go up to the roof. Because that was the only way we could see what was going on. I mean, even the Iraqi TV was shut down. Other than the radio, a lot of people used to listen to Monte Carlo or BBC. But we don't believe what we heard. I do sometimes, but people don't in general. Personally I don't give a fuck. So I was just, you know, going up to the roof, seeing whatever I could find, like, "Okay, this part has been taken or not, whatever, Americans here or there," I don't know. I couldn't see shit anyway, but it was a kind of like curiosity, you know, what's going on?

I was sleeping, at three, four o'clock, maybe five o'clock or something, sunfall, and my brother came to me and told me, "Wake up, the American tanks are rolling in."

I thought, It couldn't be. They can't be here. Because the last thing we heard they were like forty miles away from Baghdad. So we didn't know anything other than what we heard in the Iraqi media or what's going on in the street. I told him, "No way, that's impossible."

BULLET HOLES IN U.S. ARMY HELMETS, CROSSED SWORDS MEMORIAL, BAGHDAD
INTERNATIONAL ZONE. THESE HELMETS ARE AT THE BASE OF THE MEMORIAL.
PHOTO BY STUART GRIFFITHS.

He said, "You look yourself." I jumped out and looked. We had a
square on our street where all the tanks just gathered, and I looked at
them. I thought, That's an Iraqi tank, it couldn't be American, and he
told me, "Look at the flag they have." It was American.

At that time, I had mixed feelings: I don't know what to think.
Should I cry because it's my country being taken over? Or should I
laugh because I might be "free" now?

But I didn't feel anything; I had a fight within. You have these
feelings like, Okay, my country has been taken over.

I mean, whether you like where you live or not, it's still your
homeland. So it's hard. Imagine you're living in your house and
somebody just comes and grabs you out . . . well, not even grabs you,
just takes over your house and you can't say anything, whether you

like that person or not, or whether you like your house or not. It's just complex feelings: I was happy, I was sad, I was angry, I was just cool. So when I looked from the balcony, I didn't believe it. The first time I thought, No, that's an Iraqi tank, it might be an ambush or something and my brother just said, "Look at the flag," and a tank came rolling by, crashing over the concrete barriers, just crashing over and they have the American flag on. It was just like, "What?"

MARWAN: I remember the night we went to my aunt's house; the bombing was not so bad down there. They lived in the city center and my house was more East Baghdad. We traveled together, my family. It was close to my cousin's music store. We went there in an old Russian car. They already had five families in one house. I used to go to the top of the roof; my cousin had birds. It was the same cousin who sold me the drums. Pigeons and stuff like that. He used to sell them, made a living that way, because the music store wasn't enough. I sat up there and there were the bombs. I saw fighters shooting missiles. They told me that I was crazy to go on top of the roof while a war was happening but I couldn't bear it down there in the house. It was like a mental hospital, with twenty to thirty people going crazy, having panic attacks, kids screaming, and mothers helplessly trying to shield their babies and children with their bodies. It was overcrowded, total madness.

Everyone knew what was happening, even the babies. It was war. But after all, this is what happened, we passed it and we were alive, but not everybody made it. I remember on the day that Baghdad was invaded, I didn't think they were American soldiers. I remember saying, "No, they're regular soldiers, Mum." She was looking behind the curtains, she was crying, she had like a nervous breakdown, and I was like, "No, Mum, they're regular Iraqi soldiers, don't worry." I realized being in a war is one thing, but being invaded is another. All this time we were oblivious to the fact that the infantry was reaching the city center of Baghdad because the local media weren't saying anything about it. So you can imagine how shocked we were when we heard the roaring of the cavalcade of tanks approaching our vicinity.

But one of the guys took off his cap and he had blond hair. That's when I knew.

FIRST NIGHT OF
U.S. "SHOCK AND AWE"
AIRSTRIKE CAMPAIGN
AGAINST IRAQ,
MARCH 19, 2003.
PHOTO FROM EYEVINE.

6

FIGHT FIRE WITH FIRE

FAISAL: More and more American troops were coming into Baghdad all the time. I heard an engine on the pavement and I just thought, They are coming. My aunt was staring from the window and watching them. There were my four uncles and their families, about five families, and my grandmother.

And we waited. And we played poker. And we played Risk.

Like, "I'll get your country."

"Yeah, well, they already got it, take the other one."

I practiced my new songs, too.

I didn't write any new music at that time. I never thought that things would get more intense. I heard a rumor that my mother did write in a diary, but I never read it—she hid it somewhere.

Anyway, when the Americans got to our street, some people started to go out and socialize with them.

TONY: It was an evening in April when I first met one of the American troops. I was going home from the military camp, and it was around one thirty, to be exact. I was tired; I took a shower and ate. I slept until four or four thirty in the afternoon and then my mum woke me up—she told me the American tanks had arrived. They had invaded Baghdad. I didn't believe her, because I'd just got back from the military camp. When I went out, I saw them with my own eyes, and the first thing that came to my mind was "Sad but True" by Metallica. I didn't talk to the soldiers. Everything was a total mess. For a second, you feel everything you know about your country is falling apart before your eyes, a whole culture. You just stop thinking, actually, because everything is happening too fast. A whole leadership changed from night to day, and probably the whole system and the whole culture will change, too. But who am I to think about these things? I'm just a musician. We have a saying in Iraq: "The news that sells for money today, you can buy for free tomorrow."

FIRAS: I met some American soldiers in the street and we talked. The first impression they got, a lot of them thought I was from America or something. The first soldiers I met, a couple of them were marines. I don't know which unit, they wouldn't tell you, so I sat and talked to them, and you know, got to know them, like a real person: "What's your name? Where are you from? What do you do?" One guy kept looking at me and he finally asked me, "Who are you working for?" and I told him, "I work for nobody."

He said, "Where are you from?"

"From Baghdad, originally."

"You're an Iraqi?"

"Yes."

"But who do you work for? I thought you were press."

"No, I'm just a regular person."

"Then what the hell are you doing next to me? Get out of here!"

It was fucking funny, and he couldn't believe that I'm just an Iraqi citizen and thought I was trying to get a news story or something.

Sometimes when they do patrols, and they see you wearing a metal T-shirt, they might be like, "YEAAAH, METALLICA!" They like that shit; they were excited to see that. They set up in different neighborhoods, staying there for a week or so, and there was certain confusion happening with the locals. They didn't know if they should be friendly with the Americans or just turn against them and that would be the typical conclusion of being occupied.

FAISAL: My first contact with the Americans was by having an argument with some soldiers. They have this heat-seeking system in their tanks, to detect bombs and stuff, and I was getting hot bread from a bakery. As I walked past them, their machine gun just went toward my bag. It was a hot summer night—it was as hot as hell and that plastic bag was melting, so they thought I was carrying something dangerous. There was a tank, standing there blocking the street.

And one of the soldiers just flagged me down and said, "Son, let me see in your bag."

I was like, "Are you talking to me?"

"Yeah, I'm talking to you."

I said, "It's not your business."

"Are you trying to pick a fight?"

"I'm not trying to pick a fight, but it's not your business."

"Open the bag."

"No."

"Open the bag!"

"No!"

"You speak English, right? Open the fucking bag!"

"It's only hot bread!"

"Let me see it!"

We kept saying that for about half an hour until one of the majors said, "Okay, what's the fucking problem here?" The soldier told him, "I asked him to open the bag and he refused."

"Why did you refuse?" his superior said to me.

"Because it's none of your business," I said back.

"Open the bag or there will be consequences."

"Are you threatening me?"

"Yes, we're threatening you."

So I opened the bag and was like, "Want some?"

They were staring into the bag and it was a strange shape of bread. They said, "What is that?"

"It's bread, smell it. You can eat it. You can feed yourself with it."

"Is that bread?"

"Yeah, it's healthy. It's an Iraqi one. It's delicious, very delicious. You take it."

"No, I can't take it."

We argued again and again. "You have to take it," and so finally he did.

He was just a kid, my age or maybe younger. He couldn't have been older than twenty-one. I never saw him again after that, because they switched patrols every day, maybe every couple of days. The bakery, though? I'd go in every day for supplies for the whole family. The bread was great.

We started socializing with the troops more. Iraqis started socializing with them, trying to figure out a good way to go about with them around, and they were nice. And they acted good. The first year or two years, they acted well. They negotiated well. After that, things started getting nasty on both sides. I don't know who started it.

MARWAN: Right after the war, I met an American soldier myself. In all the chaos that was going on, some people robbed and burned down a tax office near my aunt's house, where we were staying. There were four or five younger guys coming toward my dad, trying to attack him, so I tried to push one of them away. My dad started threatening people with a stick. I blacked out and started pushing them, starting an argument; some people were too blind to see they were robbing their own country. It was chaos down there. And these guys were threatening us with "the new authority." You see tanks and you see a guy riding a horse, you see a guy carrying flags and a guy pulling a refrigerator. Insanity. I went down there and tried to talk to the American soldier who was watching all this happen, to ask him for protection, but the situation was so intense, I couldn't speak English. My dad stepped in and *he* talked with the soldier, said that within all the chaos that was happening, maybe the Americans should offer more security for the people and the soldier replied by saying that he was just in charge of that specific spot and he had specific orders and he couldn't do anything about it.

Some people were cheering for the American soldiers, some people were still trying to get their injured ones to the hospitals, and others were busy robbing what they used to refer to as "war spoils." My dad and I just went back and we decided to leave my aunt's house, because it wasn't safe anymore, and go to my cousin's house instead. That was serious frustration. I guess we were on the run even before we became refugees. On the run in our own homeland.

FIRAS: I could see American soldiers out in the street. I went to just look at them, not to meet them. They weren't in the mood to meet anybody—they were as confused as we were, is how I would describe it. They were just playing their role of guards; they didn't act friendly or offensively, they were just soldiers. There was this humongous marine tank, just huge. I saw the army tanks and stuff, these are even bigger. I was impressed, you know. Like when they open the hatch, you see all the people running just to see what's inside the tank, what it looks like inside. When the Americans came with their helmets and body armor and all the technology they got, they looked like aliens coming from space. Like, what the fuck? Some people believe they had these X-ray glasses where they can see people naked or stuff like that.

There were women hiding because they didn't want the soldiers to X-ray them. I knew there was nothing like that, but the old folks didn't, and people, they were really curious anyway, you know, they wanted to talk to the Americans, even those who don't speak English wanted to give them flowers, give them chocolate or something like that.

Some people were happy that these guys were here, and of course some people were not. I was neither—I wasn't happy or sad, I was just looking at everything with hollow eyes. Like I'm just seeing pictures, my brain is not working, it's not functional. I was depressed, happy, I was crying, sad, and laughing, just a fucking mix of feelings. Because you might question whether they were coming here to help us or not . . . but still, I'm glad that they came, kind of. They tried to help us . . . but then again, I'm not glad they're here. So . . . I don't know what to say about it.

I saw the statue of Saddam being pulled down—I was a hundred meters away. It was a sad moment, very sad really. Because whether you liked that person or not, he was representing our country for more than three decades. It's a matter of who you are—this character, Saddam, had become a symbol for the country and he was a part of our lives whether we agreed with him or not. I was literally paralyzed. Looking at things happening in front of me and not realizing what the hell's going on. Everything was confusing. When they pulled the statue down, I didn't know whether it meant good or bad or whatever.

I didn't know it was going to happen. I just saw people walking

BROKEN AND ABANDONED BRONZE STATUES OF IRAQI MILITARY HEROES
FROM THE IRAN-IRAQ WAR AT THE ARTS DIRECTORATE IN BAGHDAD.
PHOTO FROM EYEVINE.

down the street so I went with them; I wanted to see what the hell was going on, because people were cheering, and some people were just like me. I saw what happened, and I went home and started crying. That was the only way to get my anger out—I cried, for real. And I was thinking, What the hell will happen? I didn't care about anything. I don't know, but I was really depressed, so I went home and just started fucking crying, and that's the only thing I could do. I don't have the power to tell the American troops what to do, I can't do anything. I can't fix things.

I couldn't talk to the guys in the band. I was sleeping in my room, and we didn't have cellphones at the time, so we couldn't contact each other, other than at the local phones, but some of the areas were already bombed, the phone stations were bombed.

I saw the rest of the group a couple of weeks later. Marwan came to stay with me. He felt the same thing. I mean, no comment, you've got nothing to say about it.

FAISAL: We noticed things getting worse—a lot of forced searches, a lot of neighborhood searches. American soldiers weren't used to being polite. When they want to search a house, they enter without any notice. They don't care, you know. Sometimes they smashed doors down. They started getting confused.

That was the biggest mistake, I think. People started resenting them and the situation just because of that, and they didn't know what to do.

My own house was searched while I was in there, but not in the same way. After a while, after the Iraqis had joined the American army, the Iraqis would start going into people's houses and apologizing first and saying, "Okay, do you have some weapons? You better show us them now before we search, because if we do and we find something, there'll be another consequence to this. So you better tell the truth right now," and for real, I told them I didn't have any weapons.

From when I was born until now since we owned that house, we never had any weapons inside the house.

And I was there when they searched my family home. I was alone actually, because my family was out on their work day. I was asleep; I'm a very heavy sleeper. It was about half past twelve, noon. I was sleeping in the living room because on the second floor there was no electricity and I was half naked because there was no fresh air. They went through the middle garden, in the middle of the houses. I just freaked out like, "What are you doing?!"

And all I could see was a bunch of guys in uniform, waving guns. I was yelling, "Whoa, whoa, whoa, chill out, guys!" then I ran into the kitchen. The kitchen contains the front door and when you open the door, there's the garage, and then the big gate. But they'd already gone through the big gate. They'd figured out some way to open it. They started asking me, "Where were you? Why wouldn't you open it?"

"I was asleep."

"Where is everybody else?"

"Out."

"Okay, do you have any guns?"

"No."

"Are you sure?"

"Yep."

Then an American soldier started talking to his Iraqi interpreter, asking him to translate and he said, "You tell him, if he's lying to us and won't cooperate, there are going to be serious consequences."

I heard that and I got really upset because I was telling the truth from the beginning. I reacted instinctively, "Say what? Maybe I've scrambled my brains from the sleeping. If you want to say anything to me, say it directly. I told you I don't have any weapons, okay? Why don't you just get over it? If you want to search, be my guest. Show some respect. You're in my place." He just kept staring at me. I don't know whether he wanted to believe it or not. Am I actually speaking English or not? And I actually sounded like one of them.

He kept doubting me. But I just sat on the stairs and told them to go ahead. He explained, "We're not an occupation army! We're here to do different stuff and keep people safe!"

"Okay, well, thank you very much, but beyond everything . . . don't talk to me about politics. I'd hate to argue with you about politics, because I've got theories and you've got theories. I've got a *way* different perspective of all this than you do. So don't argue with me."

"No, let's talk about—"

"No, I don't want to talk about it, you've got your job to do and I've got my job, and I want to get some sleep, so I can get back to it."

I went to the guy afterward and apologized. You know, I had proved my point already, I didn't have any guns, and I went to him and I told him, "Listen, I'm really sorry. I know you had a bad day and I really had my own day for it, so please don't really be mad."

He said, "It's okay, man. Don't worry about it."

We were searched a couple of times but just normal searches. You know, "Put your hands up!" and they search you.

MARWAN: We learned not to think about the reasons, because there are no reasons and nothing to justify it. The reasons why they bombed Iraq, the reasons why Iraq became such a bad environment after it had been one of the leading civilizations of this world, the reasons why Iraq got to this situation in the first place, the reasons why I started working when I was eleven, the reasons Tony's dad had been a war prisoner for eleven years, the reasons why we're refugees now and are exiled. What did we do?

There is no one to blame. Blame who? You, me, the government, the people behind it? If you try to blame people, you'll end up hating them. Every time you see someone having fun, every time you see someone having a birthday, every time you see someone being re-united with their family, every time you see someone having a decent life. You start thinking about your family and what you are leaving behind, the warmth of home, and at what cost? All your friends and memories are scattered all over the globe, because each and every one of them had fractions of it. Like when you see people down the street dining for like a hundred dollars; well, this hundred dollars can last a fucking month.

This is why we play music. We don't want to go and break people in two. Because I'm telling you, there are a lot of people who deserve that, but there are a lot more of them that don't. They just need someone to show them the way. We're not paragons or anything—we're just people who happen to be in the wrong place at the wrong time (that's a nice way of putting it), and there are many, many just like us. But we are lucky now, to have the choice to make a band, to

A PRIVATE SECURITY CONTRACTOR EN ROUTE TO BAGHDAD INTERNATIONAL
AIRPORT, DECEMBER 2005—THIS SECURITY COMPANY IS A "LOW PROFILE"
SECURITY OUTFIT—THEY FEEL BLENDING IN IS BETTER THAN BEING HIGH PROFILE
BECAUSE IT CAUSES TENSION WHILE DRIVING OUTSIDE THE INTERNATIONAL ZONE.
PHOTO BY STUART GRIFFITHS.

have the option to do that, and to continue. We're lucky enough to
have the strength. We were fortunate enough to hear our parents'
stories about how Baghdad had been, but not fortunate enough to
live it. We had to live in the nightmare, wounded Baghdad. I remember while growing up that my dad used to tell me the sky was the
limit. I remember everything about these dreams that I once had,
which had vanished bit by bit. I had all these visions that one day
would come when I would be the man that I wanted to be. I still remember the nights of Baghdad, me and my family and my friends,
traditional stories of how great Baghdad had been once upon a time,

things like *One Thousand and One Nights*, how the civilization started and the people were treated, how the Tigris flows into this beautiful city and how people were dumping dead bodies in there now. Bodies that were never taken out. I guess this is our legacy and heritage now.

FAISAL: As things went on, Baghdad became more and more dangerous. I had to cut my hair and grow a beard, just because of how society had become, because it was dangerous if you didn't fit in. The militias can kill you for it, the death squads, you know.

People started asking for their own rights as civilians. Some of them were out of the country and they came back like they had been there for years. They were forced out. The militas started re-creating their old nonsecular neighborhoods. Threatening a lot of people who wanted to leave, taking advantage of a lot of people, taking revenge. Anyone who stood against them or said something about them or cooperated with the regime, just to take them out. And now these people, they were taking their own revenge. They started convincing even the young men to join their troops. They told them that it's for a good cause, but there are lots of other causes, as well. Like kidnap and extortion and torture. And some of them leave their jobs and join these militias. They leave or are turned in by their families. Or they will enjoy killing someone's family one by one.

I saw a lot of people receive death threats and be forced to leave. My neighborhood, especially, a lot of the surrounding neighborhood. They had been there for years and just because of their religion, they were forced to leave. All the occupation/invasion did was bring in more laws.

MARWAN: I remember writing the lyrics to "Message from Baghdad" the day me and Faisal were almost killed by a car bomb.

I was going downtown to the practice space we used to have, then went to see Saad and check the basement out and see how it's going down there. It was kind of like a regular day for us—we came out, I'd parked my car by the building. I was planning to leave Baghdad for Syria but I told Faisal that I should say good-bye to Saad before I left.

So we went down there and I said good-bye to him. We went back in the car and the minute that I put the keys in to open the door, the bomb went off about twenty meters away—it was that close, and I remember that I actually saw the bodies flying up, because it was a crowded area, as well, a crowded neighborhood. The bomb went off, I saw the sparks, I felt the pressure, I felt the blast and the heat, and I saw the bodies and the construction at the side of the road flying up in the air—this is something I'll never forget. I didn't find Faisal; he had dropped on the side of the road because of the blast, then he disappeared, so I was worried about him. You need to understand all this happened in one minute, or less—a matter of seconds. I was wearing sunglasses and they fell off so something happened to my eyes, as well, and I could still see these monstrous flicks of the explosion.

So we went back, closed the car door, started running back, retreating back to the building, because we'd heard when one bomb goes off another two or three would at the same time, a whole series. We went down in the practice space and at the same moment, Faisal's brother called to tell him he had a newborn baby. So we gave him our congratulations and stuff—we didn't tell him actually that the bomb went off, and he was so happy, so we talked to him for like ten minutes, right after the explosion. Our voices were shaking, because we hadn't even had a chance to talk about what had happened before the phone rang, but we had to repress it. So that was it, and I told Faisal that if it wasn't for the hugs and good-byes for our teacher, we probably would have been in the middle of everything when it went off. I remember going back home, still feeling my body shaking. I know the road, I know how to drive, so I did it, but I didn't really think about it because my mind was stuck in that moment and I believe it will be forever.

The same night I started "Message from Baghdad," because a friend of mine is a reporter and the name came from when one day I was sitting with him, and he wrote something, for reporters or whatever, and he wrote the title "Message from Baghdad" and I was like, "Why did you write that?" He told me, "Whenever you send a message, and you want to make sure everybody in the industry wants to read it, you should write 'Message from Baghdad,' everybody is going to read it."

I wanted to make my experience there reachable for other people. Hopefully they'll get to see what happens, from my eyes, or the eyes of the people who have been down there. Suddenly all these events we'd been through came rushing to my mind, and I had to put them down on paper. Something had to be said or done. This is the way I channel my anger and fear.

FAISAL: The main thing I want to do is tell people who don't know, who didn't see the war, that the main thing was the kids. There were bodies of a lot of kids in the streets. And when you see that, you just feel everything is finished, you know? You just feel that all these words that had been said on the radio by the Americans—that "we are here for you"—was a bunch of lies.

I didn't even know what it was all about. I see my people and my friends going through war. Why? For what? I just want to know what is it all for? It's not like my parents told me what it was for. It's not like my friends had been trying to convince me that it was a good thing. And I still don't understand it. I just don't know whether it's going to last or not. All this chaos and bloodshed everywhere you go. Is it going to finish someday? It's been already five or six years . . . Someday I'm going to get married and have children, and I want to go back to my homeland. I'm not talking about tomorrow, it doesn't have to be tomorrow. I just want to figure that there will be some day that I can go to Iraq again to see my family and friends and my neighborhood without getting killed.

Now it is gloomy there. You can't imagine. Now the killing has been turned into art. They've developed different kinds of torturing. Drills on the head, taking out the eyes, smashing out the throat. The death squads are doing this. And gangs. Nobody knows exactly who they are but I would hear about them all the time. When I was still there, I started to notice a lot of people missing from my neighborhood.

One day I heard some other folks saying that they kidnapped someone and tortured him to death. Afterward they called the parents and said, "If you want your son's dead body, you've gotta pay more." They even sell them the dead bodies. If you don't pay, they just send you the head. Simple.

Later on, when we left Iraq for Syria, we'd go and extend our visas on the Iraqi border and we would hear a lot of horrible stuff that will make you wish that you don't ever go back. It's creepy. For me it's like a nightmare. You can't get rid of it. You can't think about it. You can't believe it. This is what we've been through. They're a bunch of animals; in fact, they're even worse.

When I was working my last job, I used to sneak out from my house to my job and from work back to my house, even late at night, just to avoid all the eyes on me, just to stay alive. Then the killings started in my neighborhood. They started kicking out old families. Sending a lot of death threat letters with a bullet in the envelope. If they didn't move out, that bullet would get put in their head. I heard about a family who was in the middle of leaving their home, but had passed the deadline that they were given. The father was killed in the middle of the street, even though he was trying to leave. They killed the grocery guy. They killed the bakery guy. They killed the barber guy and the guys that own the CD store. They just didn't care.

They're doing this to give you a message: You wanna live? We won't let you live. You wanna die? We won't let you die respectfully.

We'll keep dragging your ass out on the street or we'll keep chasing you until you die. Or by breaking one of your parents' hearts by killing you or smashing your throat and cutting it over the phone and making them listen to it. We heard a lot of rumors and police can confirm it all the time. You know, speaking to them. Because a lot of them have been kidnapped, too.

The guys and I started meeting at the store where the practice space was. After work, I went to practice. Sometimes if I had a concert, I'd take the whole day off.

Our first practice after the bombing was before I started working for the ministry. In 2003, we were preparing for our fourth concert. It was a very simple Christian club, they had all these Christmas lights inside it. It was kind of fun to come back to some kind of normalcy. After all this devastation, it was good to finally get to see your friends and families and your band again and practice.

MARWAN: Up until late 2003, it was okay. Then what happened, I guess, was that people were in a phase of waiting and nothing bad was happening. So far so good, you know? After all they'd been through, Iraqis became numb and recovered easily. I don't know if I should say that. Maybe some are still living through an infinite hell, remembering their loved ones. I know sometimes I am. But *we* had to recover. This is the only way. It's not like there's another option.

Soon, the wheel of life began to turn again. People were going to their stores and visiting each other's houses, weddings were announced, while on the next block people were still attending funerals. It's a cycle of death, destruction, and killing, and then you move on. It's like the Iraqi song says, "We bury our own dead in the morning and forget about them by evening." That is just like a dark, ironic way of explaining how Iraqis are capable sometimes of acting oblivious to stuff.

At that time we were so optimistic that we could write and perform

A LOCAL IRAQI EMPLOYED BY A BRITISH SECURITY COMPANY ON GUARD,
BAGHDAD INTERNATIONAL ZONE, DECEMBER 2005. SOON AFTER THIS
PHOTOGRAPH WAS TAKEN, THE SECURITY GUARD LEARNED HIS UNCLE HAD
BEEN MURDERED BY THE INSURGENCY. PHOTO BY STUART GRIFFITHS.

new songs because Iraq was going to be the new Dubai or any European country, most people had an optimistic point of view. We found a new place and we began practicing there because some other people had occupied our old space. We got to working on getting ready for some more concerts.

FAISAL: It was awesome to see all the guys again after the war. I mean, Marwan and I saw [each other] a few days after—we never separated. But Tony and Firas, I was so worried about them. Because Tony lived near some ministry that would have been a target for the Americans, I was afraid they were going to bomb this ministry or one of the government apartments. I was terrified that he could have anything happen to him.

I went there with Marwan to check them out and they were okay and laughing and talking about what we saw and how we survived for a long three days. We spent the nights with each other. Sometimes we couldn't get back home because the store was so far from our neighborhood and we had to cross over the river. Our paths could've been blocked by the Americans and if one of the militias or gangs saw us getting stopped and then talking to them in English, then that would be a problem because they would consider us American-ites.

You can tell who is in a gang because they cover their head and their face. They'd just appear and disappear and reappear. Just like ghosts.

The first postwar gig was cool, but about sixty percent of the people were journalists. They wanted to see that phenomenon thing. CNN interviewed us before the regime fell, for the first time. They saw us talking English and they wanted to know what young Iraqis thought about the war. We just said, "We don't know yet. We don't know if there will be a war. We just don't believe that." And after that I started working with the press, doing translation, and I told them we had a metal band.

Then Gideon Yago found us and wrote an article, and that is how we got involved with *Vice*. In 2003, Gideon was working with Waleed Rabia and he was translating stuff for him. Waleed brought him to our practice space and that's where the photograph that ran with the article comes from.

MARWAN: Gideon was a soft-spoken guy, easygoing. He came to the practice space with Waleed and he did an interview with us. I don't remember much of the conversation, but he asked us a bunch of stuff about being in a band, and how that felt. I remember we were practicing for the fourth concert at that time. He was a cool guy.

GIDEON YAGO: I found Acrassicauda while I was working at MTV making documentaries about Iraq and we were looking to find kids to profile because we wanted to have some Iraqis on air. We found some people there who'd been part of a TV show called *Bridge to Baghdad,* which was about a bunch of Iraqi and American teens. One of the people in it was Waleed Rabia, and he mentioned to me that he had a heavy metal band.

We put him on live TV via phone so he could talk about the stuff that was going on there, but somewhere in the middle of the phone call a bomb hit the local switchboard and severed our phone conversation. Two months later I went out there myself to meet him and I ended up meeting Marwan as well. I spent the majority of the time that I was out there with the two of them.

Waleed was working for this newspaper start-up that was like a community newspaper like *LA Weekly* or the *Village Voice*—it wasn't just that these guys had this heavy metal band. And for guys who were twenty, twenty-one, twenty-two years old, they were incredibly DIY. The band was their one retention to regular, normal life. It was the one thing that allowed them to actually still be human in a life that was all framed by the war.

We knew that the band stuff was never going to make it into the MTV show we were making because we had such a limited amount of time to actually do it, and knowing it was going to wind up on the cutting room floor, I called up *Vice* and said, "Hey, do you want a story on the one heavy metal band in Baghdad?"

Despite the fact that Waleed was working as a translator, and they were all up in the thick of the war, I thought their band was one of the most interesting things about them.

I wanted to know what it was like to be living now in occupied Baghdad and we traveled around the city and did some stuff. We went down to the former Olympic HQ, which had become Saddam's personal skyscraper/torture den. That was the first time I saw a firefight between U.S. infantry and the separatists. It was just like watching a thunderstorm heading through: "Okay, let's get the fuck out of here before they start moving our way."

OBSESSIONS ISSUE OF *VICE* MAGAZINE, WHERE THE FIRST ARTICLE *VICE* WOULD WRITE ABOUT ACRASSICAUDA APPEARED, JANUARY 2004.

The Acrassicauda practice space was based in the Karadah market. It was a strip of hangout places like clubs and restaurants, sort of the social district in Baghdad.

At that point everything had really shut down. There was a curfew and you were starting to get these militias who were doing stuff like throwing grenades in barbershops. When we went down to Karadah at night, no one really wanted to be out on the streets after dark, people were getting notoriously trigger-happy at checkpoints, and you never knew who was around and what they were up to.

Their practice space was incredibly dusty. There was zero circulation and everybody was chain-smoking, so it wasn't the healthiest environment. There was some foam on the walls and whatnot but there were pieces of drywall in front of what were formerly glass windows in front of the shop that they had boarded up. They'd written "Metallica" on the walls. It felt like going into a clubhouse that you'd make out of crap with your friends in your backyard. But it was theirs. It was their little corner of Baghdad. The whole city was going nuts and it was their one oasis and their place, you know?

MARWAN: We all got together again, after the war, and we made the decision that we needed to do another concert—it was going to be our first concert after the war. I went and arranged the hall. We wanted it to be in a place that was as safe as possible. We started practicing six hours a day. Waleed was with us, too.

Then Waleed went on his own path—he didn't turn up to practice, and I guess he was applying to leave Iraq. Then he came back after four months and said, "I want to sing," and I said, "No." At that point it was either Waleed or me. I always believed the singer should be the first guy to come to the practice space and the last guy to leave. I didn't believe that you could leave for four months and abandon your guys. Plus, some misunderstandings happened between me and him. He left in the middle of us recording our first three demos. We recorded the first demo, then, for the second one, he left. So we had like full recorded demos, musically mixed, and no singer. We stayed in this situation for two months. So there was either me or Faisal to sing it, and I wrote the words, so I sang it, but I know I'm not much of a singer. By this time we didn't want anybody else to sing the songs. We wanted a member of the band, so it stayed in the family. I was already the drummer in the band—I didn't need to take anyone's place. I told him that was it, because we had made so many sacrifices and he had so little time, and arguing doesn't solve any problems. All of us were stuck about making a decision about Waleed being in the band, since we knew he wasn't going to stay in the country. It was sooner or later he was going to leave. He had his circumstances, but we had ours, too.

WALEED: I left the band pretty much just after the bombings. We had a bit of a bad fallout when I left the country. I used to work as a journalist and a translator for journalists and NGOs, so most of my association was with foreigners. I was contracted to work for the BBC and so this put me in the danger zone in an extreme way.

If you're seen with foreigners, you are suspected to be a spy or a collaborator. I received a few death threats. There were three letters dropped in my house. I was staying in different places so nobody would know where I was. Working for the media was a very, very dangerous job and I didn't want to get my parents involved in that.

Occasionally I would just drop in to see them in the middle of the night. I had a couple of ID cards that would get me past checkpoints during curfew hours.

Usually I would arrive there at about midnight and leave about 6:00 A.M. so I could be at work at 7:00 A.M. The day I received my first death threat I had left at about 8:15 A.M. because I had arranged to meet somebody at my station at that time.

When I left the house, I found the letter waiting for me at the courtyard. I picked it up and opened it. It said something like, "We're going to cleanse our land from filth like you. You shall never walk again. You are a spy and an infidel." It was signed by "the killers of those who betray" and it was written in red ink and it had a stamp on it with two crossed swords. It ended with "Allahu Akbar," which means "God is great." I'd received so many death threats to my face at that point I didn't take any notice. People were generally angry that guys like myself were hanging out with foreigners. I was working with independent journalists on stories about the war. But the people of Baghdad didn't find it too cool. After the first letter, I laughed. I honestly laughed. With my job I was used to dealing with death the whole time. My job was about breaking news. Anytime there was an explosion I would go down there to see what happened.

The way to do work as a producer is to have networks everywhere, so you either pay people or you rely on friends to tell you what's happening in each and every neighborhood. You just take a flak jacket and a crew and head straight to that place. I had informers in many areas in Baghdad.

Anyway, a week later I went to my parents' house at about 9:30 P.M. and left at about 6:15 A.M. I didn't really have my own place—I was sharing with friends, or three nights a week I'd be sleeping at the station.

And I found almost the same letter again in the same place. Now I lost it. I lit a cigarette and then burned the letter and I was screaming at the top of my lungs to whoever had sent the note. At the time I had a nine-millimeter pistol and I remember firing it into the air. Like, "Come and get me. If you're a man, then come and deal with this like a man. Come and show yourself." But nobody showed up. I just didn't know what to do. It wasn't like there was a government that I could go to for protection.

Then I got the death threat by email in an Internet café near my work at Al-Koukh. The email was what finished it for me. I knew they weren't amateurs because they sent an email that couldn't be traced. They were dead serious about it.

I went to the station and discussed it with my boss and he suggested something that, it was well intended, let's put it that way. He said I should try and reintegrate myself into the community. I was like, "I'm out of here, my friend. I'm leaving Iraq." Three days later, I was in Jordan.

At the time there were no passports. The only official travel documents were something that was sanctioned by the Coalition Provisional Authority. You got this piece of paper and you could go to Jordan or Syria.

When I told the others I was leaving, we had a complete fallout. I suspect they did not believe me about the death threats. They just thought I wanted a way out of the country, which was true to a certain

SUICIDE BOMBER TARGETS, MUSTANSIRIYA UNIVERSITY IN BAGHDAD.
PHOTO FROM EYEVINE.

extent, but there was no future for me in Jordan. I was running off to save my life. But Marwan said, "You're going to Jordan. You're leaving the band."

And I said, "This is no joke. This is serious. They're really after me. I'm going to end up like Omeed. He got shot at point-blank range."

Marwan and Faisal spent the last night with me at the house the night I left to Jordan, which was April 24, 2004. My family didn't know it was going to be my last night. I didn't want my mother to know because she would freak out. She would die. So it was a secret. My family thought I was going on a training trip paid for by the BBC.

The only ones who knew were Marwan and Faisal. They thought

I was running away 'cause I couldn't take it anymore. I couldn't understand how they didn't believe me.

Anyway, two months after I got to Jordan they told me they were recording some songs and saying that it was going all wonderful. I was feeling bad and jealous because I wanted to be with those guys, 'cause we never really recorded anything when I was still in Baghdad.

MARWAN: After we met Gideon and the story about "the heavy metal band from Iraq" came out, we had to face a lot of media. There are some bloodthirsty vampires that just want to interview you and squeeze all the information out. What I hate is that they step on the same wound again and again. If you have someone that died for you that you really care about, you aren't going to want to talk about it again and again, but they want news and headlines out of it. They just keep treading the same path because it sells. They would ask everyone about death threats and we just want to move on and every day you have the cameras in your face. I don't want to talk about my cousin who died or my family, I know they are okay, probably, but that is my living nightmare every day: that I left them behind and you still have this little dark nagging dot in your soul that gets you every day that makes you blame yourself and that it is all your fault. At first we were happy to be doing interviews and speaking and practicing English even more and seeing how their world looked. Attracting attention. I remember one show there was even a reporter on my drums and I was like, "Can you get off? I can't play." Many times you will see us carrying all of our gear across the city and it is hard, we have that saying that "even the donkey is pissing blood" because it is so hot and we just take it and move it and stuff gets smashed in the process and some of the people that were filming all that were really into their job.

One day we went to this hotel and there was this guy who kept

SADDAM HUSSEIN POSTERS ON SALE AT THE CROSSED SWORDS MEMORIAL,
BAGHDAD INTERNATIONAL ZONE. THESE PICTURES OF THE FORMER LEADER
OF IRAQ ARE NOW TOURIST ITEMS ON SALE FOR THE MANY CONTRACTORS
WHO OPERATE IN IRAQ. PHOTO BY STUART GRIFFITHS.

calling us "kids," so I threw a drumstick at him and the people from
an Arabic channel had to restrain me. We just got out of a war, one
of us was a soldier in the war, two of us were teachers—I don't want
to be called a teenager or a kid. They tried to justify it by saying that
it's just his way, but you know, you are in Iraq, you should be going
by our ways. Finally they just shut us up by giving us a load of food.
Another time, these guys asked us to play music and I borrowed stuff
from my cousin and the amp burned out and they wouldn't get us
transport, the whole day, a lot of money that we couldn't afford. They
don't want to know about whatever problems you have.

Anyway, after Waleed left I told Faisal he had to sing and he was
like, "I'm not a singer," but I told him we needed him to do it. The
only guy that I could think of that was suitable to sing in English was

him. I can't sing. We're not playing pop music; we're playing fast music. So I told him, "Pick up your guitar, you start singing." We took Ahmed from a band called Semidead, a project he started on his own. He wanted to have a band but something happened with the other two members. So he started making music himself on the computer. He was a talented guy, musically. So we told him, "You know what, if you need a band we're going to offer you that." I guess it was Tony's idea for him to be in the band. So Faisal became the singer.

WALEED: One merit I would give to Saddam is that we were able to see through this bullshit and not be as gullible as the Americans about all this. I worry about the rest of the guys going to America because the only people they've met from that part of the world are people like [directors] Eddy [Moretti] and Suroosh [Alvi], who are smart. They've still not met Joe Six-Pack at McDonald's talking about "poor Afghani women being oppressed" while he's beating his wife every night. They're going into a country where the number one movies are things about talking fucking Chihuahuas.

I feel angry. There is a poem by Virgil where he talks about Rome being attacked by the barbarians and he says:

Had I a thousand tongues, and a thousand lips, and a speech
Fashioned of steel, sin's varying types I hardly could teach,
Could not read thee the roll of the torments suffered of each.

1. Intro (A-Acrassicauda A))
2. Youth of Iraq
3. The Doll
4. Psycho
5. Man of Miracls
6. Since you're gone
7. Masscar
8. Poison tree
9. My Love
10. Mosthavious
11. Dont go far away
12. For ever
13. Set me Free
14. Fly.
15. Waiken By the Rain
16.

INCOMPLETE SET LIST FOR ACRASSICAUDA'S FIRST SHOW, 2005.

TRAIL OF TEARS

FIRAS: In 2003, a lot of people were hurt in the bombings, and we still don't know if it was better or worse than '91. But everybody started looking forward, and so did we. We got together in 2004 and we made another concert, in January, like five months after the war.

In Iraq we had to play a different style because we were the only ones playing live shows, so we played anything from, let's say, rock to death metal. But later on that year, we started to build up our character as a band and pick up our own style. We wanted to play faster and harder, more aggressive. We had to stop compromising.

The environment was *the* only inspiration that we had to write the lyrics from, and that was the main influence to write the songs because all the lyrics, everything, is part of our life. You can check the lyrics. It's our life. We just talk about facts and reality. I mean, you can't feel that everybody else in the world hasn't experienced a war, because every country's been in a war somehow, but I don't think they've experienced it as we have.

MARWAN: After the bombings and the occupation, the situation got even uglier in Iraq. The civil war started to come to the surface, and there was hate between people everywhere. There were a lot of killings, assassinations, and bombings. So we had the invasion with the robbing and the looting, then it was calm, but then it got bad again, real bad. Not even comparable to the war. You didn't know who the enemy was. I remember people bombing mosques and churches, Sunni and Shia and Christians. Everything was so chaotic. That was a real step back. But we wanted to carry on with the music and so we played more shows.

In July 2004 we played a concert, like a youth festival. We played at the hunting club. We got kicked offstage so we don't think of it as a show, but it was an experience that we'll never forget. I think the committee of the hunting club found it too crazy at the time, people headbanging. They thought they were getting out of control, and they would wind up smashing the place up. But the truth is, they were just letting go of their frustrations and channeling their anger. We were playing "For Whom the Bell Tolls," and they asked us to calm everyone down. We told them it was all under control. So they stopped us on the fourth song, which was "Between the Ashes," and told us to leave the stage. We had to give a whole speech to the crowd before they shut the mixer down. We talked about how so-called democracy had been a big failure and didn't exist. After an argument with the people at the hunting club and trying to calm the angry audience down, and with our heads bowed in shame, we left.

You hear that you are free now, and you can't even play rock. So where's the freedom there? I don't see it.

FAISAL: The place was full of different kinds of sports facilities like swimming pools and tennis courts, soccer fields, and a gym. It was a very huge club.

It had a very big stage in the gardens. And we were so excited because they were offering us a good opportunity. It was like a Woodstock feeling, being on this huge stage in a garden. The promoter gave us ten tickets for free to give to whoever we liked, friends or family or whatever. And we actually invited a lot of friends, and about a hundred and fifty people showed up. It was kind of a youth arts festival and they weren't used to the kinds of songs that we played. But we had already agreed to do it and so we did.

There were many people waiting passionately to come to one of our concerts again, because they'd heard that we'd kept going despite the invasion. Our friends and fans, it was like they had been sitting down doing nothing, like they had been rusting. They just want to attend and rock out.

We were the opening band and Mohammed, the organizer of the concert, asked if we wanted to make something especially for the festival, so we created a song. He had requested something simple, more like an opening intro with a melody, and so we agreed. But as we started the song, all of our fans started running around, headbanging. All the other people who didn't know Acrassicauda got terrified. They were probably thinking, *What* the hell are you?

When they started asking us to calm everyone down, I realized that Mohammed was sneaking behind Marwan's back to tell him to lower the noise and make them sit down because, "This is not a bar or something, this is a very decent and respected place." Marwan said, "So what are you saying, that we're not respected enough to play? You asked us and you told us we could do anything."

He said, "Yeah, but I didn't imagine it would be this kind of music."

"Dude, you saw us three or four times, and you should know by now what kind of style we play!"

"Yes, I did see you before, and believe me, I admire and support your music, but this place is giving me a hard time and has strict rules. I told you that you could jam and I thought you could have some fun, but the crowd is too intense for the management of the club. I'm just an employee. I don't have any authority."

We told the audience what happened and Marwan kept screaming in the microphone, "This is bullshit!"

MARWAN: When he told us to stop playing I felt like I wanted to choke the guy. Choke everybody there. He told me to stop, and he wanted to shut the mixer down, but I told him I'd smash the mixer if he did. Then I did the speech. I didn't think about it much, sometimes I regret some of the stuff I said, but there was always a camera guy who will keep it in memory. That's what happened. We got to play three songs but we'd prepared like thirty. People were getting hyper and getting really into it.

All that democracy gimmick was just a lie. The situation wasn't going to get any worse. So that's the point when I thought nothing was going to happen, in terms of the band, and got really pessimistic. The anger was overwhelming but the guys got really depressed, they took off their guitars, leaving the amps with the sustained feedback.

FAISAL: And we finished playing and everybody just stood around, kind of dazed, wondering what had just happened.

A lot of friends started screaming and swearing at the managers of the club. Some of the people who were screaming were actually members of the club itself and it's a very decent place to be a member of.

They were pulling out their membership cards and smashing

them on their faces and then throwing them on the stage. They said "Fuck you!" to the club. They were really hardcore. That is what I really respect about our audience—they were tough and really honest about their feelings that night.

Anyway, that night we got really depressed and we were cursing every single moment that we agreed to play that concert. But eventually we realized that we had so many friends come out to support us, and that they were on the run as much as we were, so we actually gained from that experience and we realized that getting shut down was nothing to be ashamed of.

At least now I knew who my real friends were and who could support me, who could be trusted and depended on.

TONY: The club was not used to such an atmosphere like the one that we created. So when we played and we had our fans at the front, who broke and smashed stuff and took their shirts off, they freaked out. Our audience have a kind of thirst for our concerts, so when they come down they're superhyperactive—when the club managers saw the headbanging and stuff, they'd never seen something like this before. So they didn't let us finish the concert. We'd practiced five months every day and every night, so when you put in such an effort we wanted to show the people the stuff that we'd worked hard to nail. It was the first time this happened to us, and hopefully the last. We always felt repressed but never onstage. This is the only time we can really be who we are. I believe that for a moment they stripped our identity when they told us to get off the stage.

FIRAS: In 2003, we got a threatening letter. It said: "You are Americanized, playing Western music. You either quit or you will be dead." I wouldn't say that we weren't afraid. We were intimidated, but at the same time, the circumstances were different. When we got the threatening letter the situation wasn't that bad yet. You still couldn't

TOP: ACRASSICAUDA IN THEIR BAGHDAD PRACTICE SPACE, CIRCA 2005. MARWAN IS WEARING A GAS MASK HE FOUND ON THE STREET AFTER THE WAR. PHOTO BY GIDEON YAGO. MIDDLE: FIRAS HOLDING A METAL CD THAT SUROOSH AND EDDY BROUGHT HIM. [STILL FROM *HEAVY METAL IN BAGHDAD*] BOTTOM: SUROOSH ALVI INTERVIEWING THE BAND IN MARWAN'S BASEMENT IN SYRIA, 2007. [STILL FROM *HEAVY METAL IN BAGHDAD*]

tell who was on what side. We cared; we started to randomly change the practice time. We didn't want to get hurt, but also we thought that it was a joke, we thought it was a letter from some other jealous guys who didn't want us to play. It was a good way to avoid thinking the worst.

Practicing was hard, because we didn't have electricity, we had to have a little generator, and the generator would break or we wouldn't have money to pay for fuel. Then we couldn't practice because we had to pay the rent for the practice space.

There was not that much work at that time, because after the war everything was shutting down. The market was running low; the only thing you could sell or buy was just food and cigarettes and basic needs. I was working in IT, I fixed computers and stuff, but there was no work at that time. I was just living off my savings, and the guys, they did the same. But later on after the war, things started kind of moving again, like we'd find work.

FAISAL: After getting an education I started working with a trading company, which is owned by a big tribe. They were nice guys, loaded. It's a kind of family . . . they have this trading company, they deal with external stuff, and I worked for them for about three months. After that I started planning a new job. I practiced journalism and photography for about five months. I worked for the media. You had to go through every shitty neighborhood that had already been through war or ambushes, so I needed to figure out a place to settle down and work in an office. So I found a friend whose mother used to work in an office—they were searching for a translator, so I applied and ended up getting the job. I worked as communication personnel between the ministry and the Americans, just to make everything easier between them. A lot of different kind of jobs, it was for a good salary, and I had to help support my family somehow. It was a good job, in an office. In 2005 I worked at the same ministry but I changed

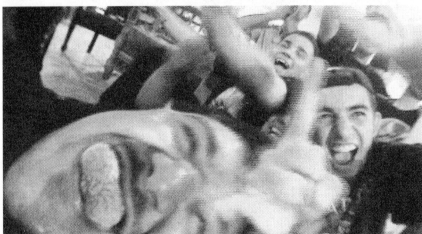

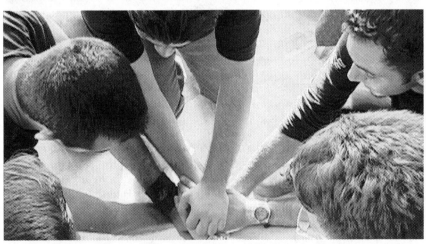

TOP: AFTER A SHOW AT THE VITALITY CLUB, DAMASCUS, 2007. [STILL FROM *HEAVY METAL IN BAGHDAD*] MIDDLE: FANS AT THE AL-FANAR HOTEL CONCERT, SPONSORED BY *VICE* AND ORGANIZED BY JOHAN SPANNER, BAGHDAD, 2005. [STILL FROM *HEAVY METAL IN BAGHDAD*] BOTTOM: ACRASSICAUDA BEFORE THE AL-FANAR SHOW, BAGHDAD, 2005. [STILL FROM *HEAVY METAL IN BAGHDAD*]

to a photographer for the administration office, shooting things for
press releases.

FIRAS: After the country club show, we played at the hotel, and that
was partly organized by *Vice*. The *Vice* article was already out and
then a Danish journalist named Johan Spanner got in touch and
said that *Vice* wanted to put on a show and they would pay for it
and film it. It was like a free show and it was well attended, despite
the circumstances of terrorists and fights and police and bombs and
stuff like that.

FAISAL: That *Vice* concert at the hotel, it was really impossible to
do. Well, almost. We never thought that anyone would show up. It's
too dangerous, and in one of the bad neighborhoods, too. If you get
caught, you get killed. And what do you know? A bunch of people
showed up. Full energy. They were all wearing black T-shirts and
they were headbanging like hell.

MARWAN: The generators broke all the time and it was dangerous,
but it went really well. About seventy people turned up, most of them
fans. There was one mortar impact near the building, it had been
happening all day. As we were setting up there were mortars landing.
There was no safe area in Baghdad at the time, and this area was
kind of considered to be inside the green zone, but we called it the
red zone. There was shooting everywhere, mortars, and they were
hitting very close. Plus, it was really hot. But the concert was very
important for us so we didn't pay attention to it. We turned the
volume up to cover the noise of the bombs, and the most important
thing was that it went well, and we were together.

We all set up our own instruments and stuff, people showed up,
and I didn't think many would. But seventy people did and [that] was
a big number. I was teary eyed—these people were really risking

their lives to come and see us. Especially in such a place, it was too dangerous. So we did the concert, for like two hours, and it was a real rush. And then we thought, Well, that's it, finished. They filmed the concert, we played, and during that time we forgot about everything: the killing, the civil war, the bombs, and mortars. The music made us feel safe and relieved.

After that concert, that same year, the members of the band all started to leave Iraq separately.

FIRAS: Things were getting scarier and from that point on, life started to evolve, getting worse and worse. They started bombing mosques and churches and stuff like that, and then the sectarian violence started to go off. Well, at least you heard that, but it wasn't religious or ethnic, just political, like who controls what. It was like the mafia, they wanted to control that area. They'd kill a couple of people, blow up a couple of things, everybody would be scared, and everybody would stay at home. They gain the power, they gain control, because people submitted easily and it was hard to figure out who you were fighting.

I don't really know who "they" were because there were so many different groups carrying out these atrocities. They might kidnap people and ask for ransom. Kidnappings were a big thing.

MARWAN: Tony left first, to Syria; he said he had to go. That was maybe three months after the hotel concert. Me, Faisal, and Firas were still in Iraq. Then Firas and I got in contact. No one had seen each other after that show and it was getting real hard to reach each other. No transport, blocked streets, tense times. One of those days like eight churches got blown up. Then the mosques followed. You never knew who was doing it; all we knew was that it was among us. It was so mixed-up. We all wanted to stay indoors.

There were a lot of curfews, roadblocks, some people started getting arrested. Militias were a big reason. There were fake traffic checkpoints, war in the streets, all of these things that made it impossible to go outside, breathe, and communicate. You couldn't feel alive. Then when it became about Sunni and Shia, it got *really* ugly. You know, Baghdad is so mixed between Sunni and Shia, even from house to house. Then for me, when you start not feeling safe in your house, it is too much. But then, the militias started, and they would come into your house and take your kids, or kill them, and you were safe nowhere. Just being who you were was all it took to be threatened or killed.

FIRAS: Tony's house was hit by a mortar round and was totally demolished, and he had to try and find a better place for his family, so he went to Syria to try and find a job and a safer life. Me and Marwan, we were supposed to go after Tony. We discussed it and we thought, Let's go and take our chances. At that time we had an invitation to attend a festival in Jordan called Battle of the Bands.

So the idea was to go after Tony to Syria, practice there for a while, and then go to Jordan, attend the festival, and then back to Baghdad. But after that, I was married, my wife was pregnant, so I couldn't travel. So Marwan left a couple of months later, I had my son, and after one or two months, I talked to Faisal and we made a decision to go and follow the guys and just start things over again. We went to Syria, but we had a short time limit to attend the festival, so we couldn't afford to get a practice space; there were a lot of things to do in one week or so.

MARWAN: It was a relief to leave the civil war in Baghdad. My mum and dad were worried the whole time, and I was like the noose around their throats—they couldn't think straight with me near them. I was a young guy, so I was a target. My dad's view was that it was okay for me to bury him, not for him to bury me. He didn't worry about

TOP: RECORDING A THREE-TRACK DEMO IN SYRIA, 2007.
BOTTOM: FIRST CONCERT IN SYRIA, VITALITY CLUB, 2007.

himself—he was really sick and was half paralyzed. What more could they do for me? He had a stroke and asthma. They wanted me to get out. I could not raise a family there. The idea of the band was fading away; we still tried, but life took over. There were no rules. I lost my identity for a while, each one of us became other people for some time. We wanted families, normal jobs, to work our asses off. We were caught in the tide of terror.

When this invitation for the Battle of the Bands in Jordan came, we breathed again, we were really enthusiastic. I thought, This is our chance. So we started talking about it, and it turned out we couldn't go to Jordan because they weren't issuing a lot of visas to Iraqis during that period. Tony was in Syria, and there were many issues and no solutions. We had no practice space, the idea of a band seemed insane at that time, and they wouldn't allow us to go down to Jordan. So I said, "Let's go to Syria, meet Tony, and practice there." So I told Tony, and he was excited about seeing us guys again. It had been six months for him there and he missed us. So we just met once or twice, Firas and Faisal and me, because it was so hard to meet up. Firas's wife was pregnant. The day before we were all meant to leave to go to Syria, Faisal and Firas had their own situations and couldn't go. Faisal wanted to stay and be engaged and Firas couldn't leave his pregnant wife. So I went alone on a bus. I said good-bye to my family—it was heartbreaking. I took one small bag with clothes, a guitar for Tony, one for me, and some drum bits. That's all I had. I was planning to go for between three and six months and was hoping that the situation would calm down. I remember telling my mother she didn't have to cry because I'd be back in no time.

So I met Tony down there, the other guys didn't turn up, and the situation got much worse. So the six months became three years and counting. And I never knew it was a one-way ticket, that is my one regret—that I did not know I was leaving permanently. I just got on the bus and went to Syria with all the others who were leaving in convoys with fridges and mattresses and whatever they could carry. The atmosphere was heavy. Many people crying. They knew they were leaving for good. They were fugitives. But I had a smile on my face—I thought I was coming back in a few months with my little bags. I didn't even say a proper good-bye to my family. I was oblivious to the fact that I might never come back.

TONY: When I left my family, it was a hard thing for them and for me, but of course they care for me and they said, "Go and see what happens, go and seek your future." So they encouraged me, but it was gut-wrenching. Everything I get I always split fifty-fifty between me and my family, because they count on me financially. I'm the oldest—I had to take the responsibility and be there for them even if not in person. It takes a lot to raise a family and it's a simple matter of money to make it fall apart.

MARWAN: Syria reminded me of the impression I got from my family of how Iraq was in the eighties. Being secure, not hearing bombs, feeling normal. We always wanted to know what it would be like to feel normal. So I had peace here, but at what cost? Now I was starting from the bottom. I pitied myself; I had gone from a nice house with three rooms and a car to living in a basement with rats and people I didn't really know. I can't even imagine that any day they would be real neighbors. So I was in Damascus and starting to learn to live like a refugee. I wasn't one yet, though—I had not applied for refugee status. But it felt like it. I was an exile living in a small, cheap room. I went to visit my sister in Aleppo and when I came back after a few days there were paw prints all over my stuff. I was like, "What is that?" Then I saw the rats all over my bed. My first three months in that basement were like living hell. For Tony it wasn't so bad because he lived with his cousins.

I spent all my money I had from Iraq on that basement. For food, all I ate was one sandwich a day, for two months. I would divide the sandwich into three and have one part per meal. It was chicken liver sandwiches, the cheapest thing you could get. I remember there was a girl in the neighborhood who used to call me "the Skeleton." I went from ninety-seven kilos in Iraq and nice home cooking to seventy kilos in two months. It really screwed me up. I slept most of the time because I had no energy. My idea of fun was to go and wash my clothes. That was like my bingo night. That was it. The room was empty except for the bed. And all I had was the one bag I came with.

There was an Iraqi woman in the neighborhood who used to sometimes bring me food or a sheet to cover me, because I was using my T-shirts to cover myself during the night.

It was really cold down there. Suddenly my family sent me some money I saved and started sending me an allowance. Then like a miracle the guys came in.

FAISAL: We met a lot of people in Syria. Living there was so easy because it was not too expensive and it reminds me a lot of the old Baghdad. My family used to talk a lot about trips to Syria in the past. When Firas and I decided to follow the guys there, I was so excited to see it, and also the idea of re-forming the band was bringing me a lot of hope. It's not like I didn't go through sixteen hours of fear to get there from Baghdad, but I kept thinking it was temporary. When we reached Syria, Marwan was expecting us. We rented a mini-bus from the bus garage and we called Marwan to get the directions to the apartment. After half an hour of driving, we were there. Marwan cooked spaghetti for us and told us to crash whenever. It was a small room, like a cube, with a small kitchen combined with a bathroom. I never thought it could contain us all, but we managed. Two of us slept on the floor and Firas's wife and the baby were sleeping in Marwan's bed. We were so tired, it was six in the morning—we thought we were going to pass out for days.

ACRASSICAUDA WITH FRIENDS AND FANS AFTER A CONCERT
AT THE VITALITY CLUB, DAMASCUS, 2007.

A couple of days later, Tony showed up, and it was the first time we had seen each other in a long time. We started talking and laughing and sharing ideas about the band's future and what the next step would be in Syria. After that, we had to start looking for practice spaces, but we didn't have much time or money. We had to take care of the little budget that we had. Marwan didn't have any drums yet, just his acoustic classical guitar, and Tony had his electric one. Firas and I had our own equipment. We had to figure out how to get amps and drums.

FIRAS: When we got to Syria, Marwan and Faisal lived in the same building but in a different apartment than us. We had never lived together before, but we pretty much were now because it was two basements and one apartment. Like a house. It was fun, but sometimes not. Because sometimes you were thinking about your financial problems or your life problems, where you were and what you are and where you're headed, and it brought a lot of tension between me and the guys. If we weren't playing music we'd just fight, or argue. We're in Syria living as refugees. I mean, we became refugees because things got way worse in Baghdad, we had our families calling us and telling us never to go back, never come back. Imagine your parents talking to you on the phone and telling you that. Imagine that you are worried about your family back there, or you get a phone call telling you that someone has been killed or kidnapped.

I got that phone call—my family told me my aunt was slain, she was like a seventy-something woman and she's blind, and she was fucking slain. Some terrorist got into the house, pulled her out, they killed her, cut her into pieces, and threw her in the street. Why? Because she was helping people who became homeless after some militia kicked them out of their neighborhood and they lived in the street, so she was helping them, feeding them. And she got killed just because she helped these people.

These serial killers you read about, they have like specific things they look for. But these guys in Baghdad, like the ones who killed my aunt, I wonder if they do it for fun. I wish I could see one of these criminals and I would eat them alive. The only thing I would ask them is, "What were you thinking?"

To be honest, that could happen to any one of my relatives. And you are away and you can't go back to help them. I was just worried about my family, and until now, I don't know what's worse.

I don't speak to my family regularly—it depends if I can call them or if they can call me. Imagine if I'm away for another six or seven

BLACK SCORPION
(acrassicauda)

Rock From
The Depth
Of Hell
SAA

Kemanci ®

21.00

23.03.08

sıraselviler cad no:33 beyoglu istanbul   * tel: 212 - 293 61 00 * www.kemanci.org

, MARCH 23, 200

years. That's a hard thing to think about. Will they be alive at that time? I don't know.

Sometimes my wife would say to me, "Okay, let's go out, see the sights, that would be fun." I would tell her, "There is nothing fun. There is nothing fun anymore for us."

You lose that part of happiness from your mind—you can't really be that way anymore. You can be happy for a moment, but after that you go back to your misery, and the problem is that this is your own shit. It's your own problem and you don't have anyone to talk to other than your friends or your family and nobody can help but you. You go back to yourself, you have the music, you want to play, you want to do something, you want to be something, you want to be something to be remembered, that we have done something. To be remembered as, I wouldn't say the great heavy metal band, but as any notable heavy metal band. So, pretty much, your personality becomes like two parts, the one that wants to go home, and the other one that wants to advance into the future.

When I was in Syria I didn't feel like a refugee—it just felt like I was away, on vacation or something, but once you're away for a while, you start getting this homesick thing, which is hard.

I can't go home anymore and that is the hardest thing to deal with.

I don't know if you can imagine or if anyone can imagine what that feels like. Even if you said you did, I wouldn't believe you.

8

MESSAGE FROM BAGHDAD

In August 2006, Vice Films went to Baghdad to meet Faisal and Firas, who had not yet left for Syria.

SUROOSH ALVI: Inside I was all knotted up and just kept saying to myself, "The camera's rolling, just do your best to describe what's going on around you. Don't think about worst-case scenarios, you've only got one chance to get it right, so don't screw up."

The actual trip down the "highway of death" into Baghdad was nerve-racking, more because of what I'd heard about it than what I experienced. We'd read how the seven miles from the airport to the

SUROOSH WITH SECURITY
DETAIL, BAGHDAD, 2006.
PHOTO BY EDDY MORETTI.

green zone was the most dangerous stretch of road in the world, with roadside bombs and insurgent attacks and lots of random violence. But it ended up being pretty mellow, apart from our driver's bizarre zigzagging driving style and his slow pace, which made us more nervous than anything else. I kept thinking, The longer we're on this road, the more chance we have of getting shot at, so can we not pick up the fucking pace, please?

EDDY MORETTI: When we finally got to Baghdad, via Germany, I was freaking out. I was thinking, What are we doing here? This is fucking stupid. We had just spent so much time trying to figure out how to get there that we didn't really think where we were going. When I got on the ground, I was like, "This is no joke. This is just crazy. What are we doing here?" But that feeling kind of went away quickly, too. You're just . . . there.

What I remember most about arriving in Baghdad was walking into the arrivals area and the whole place was frozen in the early eighties or something. It was kind of falling apart and there was a real retro-modern look to it.

SUROOSH: The Baghdad airport was completely lost in time. We got our checked luggage from the conveyer belts and walked into the arrivals area, and I looked up and saw the departure and arrival boards that had the flights still listed from when it was an active airport three years prior to our arrival, before the war. It wasn't a digital screen but one of those analog flip boards like in train stations. Seeing "delayed" or "on-time" next to cities like Paris, Istanbul, Cairo, Dubai, Amman, and London was just surreal. It was a reminder of what an international city Baghdad had been at some point, and I guess fixing the board wasn't a priority after the Americans invaded.

I knew we needed security, and the only firm we knew was a company we used the first time we went to Beirut. They quoted us a price

EDDY FILMING *HEAVY METAL IN BAGHDAD*, BAGHDAD, 2006. PHOTO BY SUROOSH ALVI.

that was way out of our range, something like $8,000 per day, for two former British SBS officers who would escort us around in armored BMWs—also not the best way to maintain a low profile. We were two days away from flying in and I contacted a girl I knew who worked for Al-Jazeera, and she put me in touch with the Baghdad Reuters office, who hooked us up with an Iraqi security company called the Sandi Group. It's owned by an Iraqi Kurd named George Sandi who lives in D.C. and is friends with George Bush Sr. So while we were in Frankfurt before flying into northern Iraq I got a call back from them, about ten hours before we got on the plane. They said they could arrange everything, two armored cars, bodyguards, a translator, and so on for $5,000 for the whole week we were there. Plus, the woman who called was a young American girl from Seattle who was laughing and saying things like "We haven't lost anyone yet!" which gave me a sense of comfort. Something about arranging our security with an American woman calling from inside of Baghdad made me feel a lot better than dealing with an old English man in London.

When we landed she came to meet us, along with a guy named Spider, a very intense private military man covered in tattoos. He introduced us to our translator and fixer, Ahmed, who was a soft-spoken guy, slovenly and jolly, with a belly. He was an English teacher in his former life, and this was the only job he could get during the war. He was trying to save money so that one day he could get married. He couldn't remember the last time he read a book—he was a guy whose creativity had been killed by his circumstances.

EDDY: After that we walked into the arrivals area. Our security team was waiting for us. They were pretty high energy. There was a blonde midwestern American girl welcoming us, and she was all like, "Hi, y'all, I'm here to take care of you," but the team was really focused and serious.

The head of the security firm was an ex–U.S. military guy named Spider, and the rest of them were locals. Spider was, like, shouting, "Do you all understand me? We are now going through the green zone!"

"Err, we copy."

And then we never saw him again.

And then we walked out of the doors to the outside and, bang—a huge wall of hot air. The hottest air I have ever experienced in my life.

All our team are freaking out with guns and vests and everything and then I looked to my left and there was a taxi stand and all these beat-up old shitty Toyotas waiting for people. And all the Iraqi dudes were just smoking and laughing and waiting by their cars to pick a fare up.

BAGHDAD, 2006. PHOTO BY EDDY MORETTI.

It was such a different vibe. Like, here we are with all our security and then there are the regular Iraqi dudes in taxis. So it occurred
to me: What would happen if we went into the city in those cars?
What would *that* experience be like? For a second we thought that's
how we should do this.

It would have basically been suicide. You have to understand that
we went there at the height of insurgency activity in 2006. There were
two hundred people dying a day and eight "major events" per day as
well. I mean, that's how you make the news, becoming a casualty.
Instead you try and blend into the culture because there are people
out there looking for us, to kill us.

SUROOSH: Things felt relatively normal when we were driving around, apart from the blown-out buildings, the military vehicles, and the constant gunfire. The architecture was a combination of beautiful old Islamic buildings and mosques mixed with these massive concrete Saddam-era structures everywhere. I really liked Baghdad, and I've never seen another place like it. But it's hard to describe what things were really like in the streets because we never got to walk around in them. The week we were there was the worst violence Baghdad had seen since the war started; there were virtually no foreigners around and if a Westerner was spotted on the streets they would be kidnapped or killed on the spot, so our security kept us on a tight leash. Which was a bummer. Not being able to engage with whatever society existed out there was frustrating.

There was one move that our security guys kept doing which was on some real Wild West shit. Whenever we were driving and there were too many cars in front of us or behind us, they would just roll down their windows and start firing their AK-47s and nine-millimeters into the air, which would magically clear the cars out of our way. The psychology behind that particular move being "Stay on the offensive and you won't get attacked."

EDDY: Ahmed coached us. It was things like how to dress. There was one little gift shop where we could get gray pants and a shitty polo shirt. We would have to wear those and then they told us to walk with our heads kind of down and our arms limp to the side.

A lot of people are on Valium in Baghdad, they're chilled out. Nobody was on speed but everybody's on a downer or a depressant. The Americans brought in a lot of Valium and dispensed it. They didn't want young men amped up—they wanted them relaxed. So the main rules were: Walk like you're on Valium and carry some prayer beads and don't speak to anybody unless spoken to. A good way of getting out of conversation with anybody else was to tilt your

BAGHDAD, 2006. PHOTO BY EDDY MORETTI.

head up and look up to the sky. Then you're acknowledging Allah and you keep walking. But we never got to walk the streets. We weren't ready to fuck around, and I didn't want to leave the hotel.

We almost tried it once but we saw all these fucking cars, and then the Iranian embassy was close to the hotel and we thought, Let's just not walk around the block.

We didn't get any Valium. I wasn't on edge. I was focused. But when I got on the plane to Baghdad I collapsed because of mental stress.

We were there about seven or eight days. The routine was that you wake up early because you have to be back there for 9:00 for curfew and there's really nothing to do from 8:30 P.M. to midnight. I guess you

SUROOSH AND EDDY AT DINNER WITH THEIR SECURITY DETAIL, BAGHDAD, 2006.

get to have a shit dinner at the hotel—something with grilled chicken. There were no other guests at the hotel except one floor that was full of Chinese people. It was just a really, really weird place.

SUROOSH: As our week progressed, we became tighter and tighter with our security guys, despite the language barrier. They were used to escorting journalists from their secure news agency compound to the green zone for the Saddam trial. Then suddenly two dudes with cameras show up trying to track down some guys in a metal band. They were both amused and confused. We weren't like the other journalists they'd protected, or weren't really journalists at all. They refused to let any harm come our way so the company kept piling more and more guys on to protect us. At one point I counted twelve armed guards for the two of us.

Our hotel was where we spent quite a lot of time, and also where that bizarre swimming scene in the movie took place with the guns going off. The place was its own little world, inhabited by a few businessmen, us, a French news agency who we never saw, and also the home of the temporary Chinese embassy on the fourth floor. Whenever we took the elevators up to our floor we would hear the sound of Ping-Pong being played by the Chinese guards. We actually stopped on their floor once and tried to play with them but they weren't having us. At one point I remember swimming in the pool and the Chinese ambassador was doing laps with his machine-gun-fitted guards circling the pool. He had his glasses on and waved to me as he swam by. He seemed like a nice guy.

The hotel itself was amazing, a relic of time past. It used to be Uday Hussein's main party spot. There was a bar and a disco and squash courts but everything was closed down. The top floors of the hotel weren't being used and were also in a state of disrepair, but the elevators still went up to the top. One night after curfew Eddy and I went up and walked around on the top floor. It was so creepy. We talked about shooting a horror movie up there after Eddy had the shit scared out of him by a stray black cat. I didn't feel safe.

A few weeks after we left, the Al-Mansour was hit by a truck bomb and something like thirty people died.

It's pretty clichéd to say at this point, but life in war doesn't stop people from living; we saw people going about their normal business. Kids playing soccer, people selling things in the markets, and so on.

EDDY: The cool thing about the night is watching and listening to the city 'cause you'd see the traffic and the fires and hear the gunshots,

SUROOSH INTERVIEWING FAISAL AND FIRAS, BAGHDAD, 2006.
[STILL FROM *HEAVY METAL IN BAGHDAD*]

but what you'd really hear is this amazing sound of the low hum of generators. That was the sound of Baghdad during the war at night. You just heard *whhhhrrrrmmmm* and you would see choppers in the sky. One night the power went off in the whole city.

The whole city just went dark. I can't remember how long it was off because I don't think I saw it come back on.

I felt like the whole city was going to explode. It was just so . . . wrong. My overall impression and Suroosh's impression was that humans are extremely powerful and really destructive.

FAISAL: Nobody knows why the Americans invaded, maybe oil, but nobody knows. Not a hundred million could figure it out. I still don't understand it. And that's why we don't talk about it when we're together. We don't understand it. We don't understand how these people think. I mean, why did Iraq have to surrender? Why? Why did everyone give up everything? Why is it happening to Iraq? It's not fair, but it's just a hard time you have to deal with.

SUROOSH: Baghdad was fucked. There was a curfew every night at 9:00 P.M., to get some kind of control on the insurgency, which was in full effect. By forcing people indoors, the Iraqi police and the U.S. army could gain a temporary grip on things. So we sat in our room and watched CNN, checked emails, and made calls. The place was wired, there were journalists and diplomats who needed this technology, and the first thing the Americans did when they took the city over was wire the green zone and some hotel parts to the hilt. For a while they even had a 917 area code in Baghdad as the telecom company setting up the cellphone technology was based in Long Island.

We would sit on the balcony and watch the lights in the entire city black out, we watched bombs going off and the choppers flying by. We would listen to the gunfire and then look at each other and go, "Ummm?" Our hotel had a generator that kept the AC going and power running even when the rest of the city was blacked out.

Eddy would sit out there with the camera, hoping to catch some of these moments. We would interview each other, tell stories, talk about the horror film we wanted to make, and smoke cigarettes. The curfew forced us to work on strict time lines and make the best use of our daylight hours. I probably got more rest on this shoot than any other shoot I've been on. When we finally got home, Eddy got sick for about two weeks and I've never felt more tired in my entire life. It was constant sensory stimulus and for every day we were there it took at least two days to physically and mentally recover.

SHERATON HOTEL, BAGHDAD.
PHOTO BY EDDY MORETTI.

FIRAS: I thought Suroosh and Eddy were crazy to come to Baghdad. So when I met them, I was like, "Guys! What are you thinking? How crazy are you to come to Baghdad looking for a heavy metal band?" And I was thinking they were out of their league. I didn't know what *Vice* did until we got to know them.

So they showed up and we did the first part of the interview, and they said, "Guys, if you ever think about going to another country, just let us know. We might be able to help you somehow." At the time, we didn't even think about that, but we just said, "That's cool. Thank you very much, we appreciate it." And after that, Faisal and I thought about it, and for us, other than our families, we didn't have dreams left in Iraq. So it was a hopeless thing, and the last solution was to leave, to do my music and to get the band together. The band became part of our life, and the music is part of our life. I play, practice, come up with new stuff, and just work on it. So me and Faisal talked about it and it was such a quick decision. We said, "Yeah! We're leaving next week," and that was it. We didn't even talk about it anymore. Once we left the interview with Suroosh and Eddy, we talked about it for like five minutes, "That's it. Let's get out."

1- Instromental
2- Animoshia
3- Under World
4- For Whom The Bell tools (Metallica)
5- Between The Ashes
6- The Unholy Lie
7- Life is Just a day and Night
8- Big Gnun   (AC/DC)
9- Gardince of Stone
10- Nothing Elss Matter (MetallicA)
11- King with No Thrown
12- Messege from Baghdad
13- Skeletons of Society (Slayer)
14- The Unknown
15- Massacre
16- T.N.T   (AC/DC)
17- psycho
18- poison Tree

9

PEACE SELLS OUT, BUT WHO'S BUYING?

BERNARDO LOYOLA (EDITOR OF *HEAVY METAL IN BAGHDAD*):
It was September 2006 and *Vice* called me to cut the very first reel of
Eddy and Suroosh's footage. I got something real quick together with
a bunch of trailers. I started cutting a few of the shows, and *Heavy
Metal in Baghdad* was one of the first ones I started watching and I
asked them for the footage of what they shot before. I assembled the
original series for VBS.TV and that's what started the whole website.

I realized the story is really amazing, that this could be a movie. We needed a little bit more, but if they went and shot again for five or six days, we could definitely make a feature-length movie. We knew the band was in Syria—I had just received an email from Firas that they were going to play a show in a few days.

MONICA HAMPTON (PRODUCER OF *HEAVY METAL IN BAGHDAD*): It was the premiere series on VBS, and it was in three parts. The first one aired in February of 2007. And then Suroosh and Eddy went back when they heard that everybody was in Syria and they were going to put on their first concert there.

We cut *Heavy Metal in Baghdad* as a series for VBS and then after we had cut the third act [*Exiles in Syria*, which aired in April 2007], we were like, "This could definitely be a feature film," and so we recut it and then rushed to send a copy to the Toronto Film Festival. It was not finished at all, and we were like, "We promise it's gonna be amazing, it's really short right now, but it's gonna be totally different." It was much more similar to the series that was on VBS than to what the film actually ended up being. The film actually has more breadth to it, there's a lot more pause to it.

The film poster is an interesting topic. Eddy, Suroosh, Bernardo, and I wanted the bomb poster originally, the "shock and awe" day that Johan Spanner had shot and had sent over to us. We loved it, we thought it was perfect. That did play theatrically. Our distributor wasn't keen on it because they thought it didn't say "band," it said "war." At the time, and possibly even now, there's this absurd film world term called "Iraq fatigue," so no one wants to touch a film about Iraq because it doesn't play well at the box office, probably because people in the United States don't want to see the bad that's going on when they're trying to escape at the theater. But this movie isn't about the war.

At one point we had this concept of wrapping a guitar in the bomb

SUROOSH AND EDDY INTRODUCING THE FILM AT ITS TORONTO INTERNATIONAL FILM FESTIVAL WORLD PREMIERE, SEPTEMBER 7, 2007. PHOTO BY MONICA HAMPTON.

photo, shooting it so it would look like war *and* heavy metal. It didn't work out, but Fender mocked it up for us. We looked at a bunch of photographs from the stills that we had taken of them playing and that's how we ended up with the DVD cover of them performing. And ultimately I personally feel like that was probably a stronger cover, because people see *Heavy Metal in Baghdad* and see a band, maybe they don't know who the band is or what it's about, but they see "Baghdad" and "Heavy Metal" and a band. . . .

MARWAN AND FAISAL ON THE IRAQI SIDE OF THE IRAQ-SYRIA BORDER, EARLY 2007.

SUROOSH: When the film came out at the Toronto Film Festival in September 2007 . . . that's when a couple of things happened. One was that the Syrian government started making announcements that they were going to kick all the Iraqis back into Baghdad on October 10. So that day came up and the guys heard that and it freaked them out. At the same time, they'd received these really weird emails that were veiled death threats: "Come back and we will take care of you. Meet us in this town at this time, come home to us." They were getting those emails because we put it up on VBS, and it landed on the You-Tube homepage, got a million views in three days, and it spread like wildfire. The media picked up on it, the Arabic media picked up on it, eventually Iraqi media picked up on it. VBS outed these guys, and we had a responsibility to them.

MONICA: We were also hopeful that the guys could get over to Berlin, for the film festival. They never made it to either the Toronto Film Festival or the one in Berlin. The Berlin festival had contacted the Syrian consulate and the German consulate in Syria and said, "We're gonna make this happen, this is no problem, they'll be here." Then they realized that they had Saddam-era passports, which are not recognized, so basically they were like, "Don't even tell them to go to the embassy because those passports don't mean anything."

When we went to Toronto one of the things that we did was we set up the website and on there, we decided to create a PayPal account and started asking people to donate. We just got this massive response and people just donated like crazy and that's basically the money that helped to get the band their visas to get out of Syria and into Turkey. It was overwhelming. We would check the PayPal roster and it would grow daily, big-time.

We sent them care packages with metal T-shirts, records, and just stuff. We knew they would appreciate having anything. Firas complained about some of the music that we sent, I can't remember which band it was. We went around the office and took Polaroids of everyone and everyone wrote little notes on them. They really liked that.

BRIAN ORCE (PRODUCER OF *HEAVY METAL IN BAGHDAD*): We collected T-shirts and CDs, basically anything nonelectronic, anything innocuous that we could send that we could be sure wouldn't get confiscated, nothing with apparent value, just because I've dealt with customs for a lot of our shoots and I know what that's like, and it's not fun. So we got everything together from people in the office and we put it in a box—you can't send something direct to Syria, at least in August of 2007 you couldn't, because they are a "terrorist country." But Germany can, so we figured we'd send it there and then to Syria. We tried to get them the *Rock Band* video game and that didn't happen, but we sent them a bunch of T-shirts, DVDs, and metal magazines, which was a lot to them, you know?

Around that same time was when we were sort of doing a lot of pat-ourselves-on-the-back work with them, we had no fucking clue of how far we were from the end. We figured, "Well, the movie's made, press attention, and a film festival. Clearly that's gonna get four dudes who have a clean past . . . this is not gonna be a problem." But they needed some cash, and *Vice* isn't exactly rolling in it, so we set up a PayPal account. This was close to the Toronto International Film Festival. We were finishing the film as we were getting into that, and that was probably the busiest I've ever been in my life. And all of us—me, Monica, Bernardo, the finishing team, so to speak—would be here till around three or four o'clock in the morning almost every day. But it was exciting.

Bernardo, Monica, and Suroosh were really working on the story of it. Then we started to get a little nervous—there was a bit of a fire under our asses for that October 10 date, so every once in a while the refugee rumor mill would start churning and people would say, "We have to leave on October 10 because they're gonna start getting stricter with Iraqi refugees." I don't know how accurate that was—I know a lot of bad stuff was happening with refugees in Syria and in Turkey at that time . . . they were driving them off to the mountains and they would beat the shit out of them. In Syria they were expelling them, a lot of under-the-table stuff. A good rule of thumb with this international stuff, I began to notice, is that anything that you think could ever possibly happen, has and is. A lot of really grim, crazy stuff, and outside of the U.S. and the U.K. and countries like that, it's lawless. It's like the movies.

FIRAS: Well, the first time that we saw the film was in Syria. To be honest, since I got to Turkey, I stopped watching the film. It's just seeing your life repeat itself again . . . it's so, so, so hard and so sad.

You see all the wasted minutes and days and emotions you went through. You feel so bad for yourself. It pinpoints a lot of things that people in the West don't know about, not just Iraq or Iraqis or refugees, but about Middle Easterners or the other side of the world that everybody's just afraid of. We are just people. We are just like anybody else in the world. We wanna rock, we wanna play, we wanna have fun. A lot of people think we live with camels and tents. We live in real buildings. We got all kinds of things. I've been talking to people since I got here and some of them, they still do believe that. It is funny but sad because, you know, the Hollywood stereotype thing. When they see me talking with this accent or English or whatever, they think, like, Well, Iraqis or Arabs shouldn't speak like that, they always have an accent, they don't look white.

Anyway, I stopped watching the film for the same reason. It brings back a lot of memories that I'm trying, not to get over, but I'm trying to use to push me forward, not to put me down. I may sit and watch it once, but I don't like to see it like I did in Baghdad or in Syria because it's just . . . So far, we had it better before than now, you know what I mean? I mean, in different ways. And hopefully we have it better in the future, but I don't want to keep thinking negatively anymore. So I just try to keep myself focused, positive, keep things going on. I listen to the songs and it gives me shivers because the songs are us and the lyrics in the music are us.

MARWAN: I hated what I saw. I hated the fact that all this time we had been numb to it and thought it was okay, natural. Every event and name I had tried to forget came alive again. I couldn't take it, too many things were drilling in my brain, saying this date, this time, this person, this event. What was in the movie and not in the movie all came together. It was too much. The idea of *being* in a movie on top of that was a lot to take in. It was like a roller coaster; it took me really far down, like to the center of the earth. I was going in circles, I

BERNARDO AND SUROOSH AT THE BERLIN INTERNATIONAL FILM FESTIVAL, FEBRUARY 2008. PHOTO BY MONICA HAMPTON.

couldn't repress it anymore. A lot of times I regret it, a lot of people got offended by the way I behaved, but I think they understood, whether they had been through it or not. What I said and did, there was no mask anymore, or maybe there were a thousand masks on my face. It was a pure driving force of emotion, anger, frustration.

I watched it many times, but sometimes it still gets me. I watched it last with some friends in Turkey—they had never seen it. They had seen the feature, which is happy and fuzzy and all that, but the full movie is kind of heavy vibes. People were looking at me and patting my back to see if I was crying. I told them, "Just watch the film, don't worry about me." I told them I have to live with this film forever.

People will always remember me for that film, what I am in it. That will be how many people think of me. And a lot of that I don't want people to remember me by. It was horrifying. A lot of goofy stuff that should have been cut, a lot of editing, stuff I wished I could have said but didn't, and lots of things I said but shouldn't have. I have to live with how I am in that film. I get judged on that, not me. It's two decades in ninety minutes. It was guys who have never been filmed before.

But the movie had to come out because we didn't have much time. I guess that's how we do stuff always: in a rush, in haste. But it's still good.

TONY: I got affected by the film first, because it's my movie, and second, to see yourself in that atmosphere, and plus a lot of people worked on that movie. It's a good work, I feel privileged, I loved it.

It felt so bad to see the bombed practice space, it felt like shit, but this is the reality, but at least we had the movie. Of course it is good to present that—happiness, then ugliness.

I don't follow much of what's happened since the movie. It's always Marwan and Firas, but when they tell me this stuff I'm always happy.

FIRAS: The attention was in a good way, let more people know about the band, about the film, deliver the message that we have, which is: We are just people, we exist, just like anybody else in the world. Also how refugees live—Iraqi refugees or any other refugees in the world, but I think that Iraqis have it the worst. I don't know, maybe because I've had it like that. So it started having a bigger message than what we even thought about, which became a responsibility on our shoulders. Then instead of just rocking around, now you have to watch what you say, what you do, how you act, stuff like that. Because everything you will do will turn on not just you. It's really funny because we never thought about it like that and we never cared about it. Like, "Screw that, I can go have fun, party, drink, whatever, play a concert." It's just me, I'm not representing anybody. And yes, I want to deliver this message because it's ours as it is somebody else's. So it's part of my responsibility to do it, but in my way, with my lifestyle.

FAISAL: In the end, *Heavy Metal in Baghdad* was meant to happen because people out there need to understand that Baghdad experienced a certain period during which Iraqis had to live in the eye of the storm but continue with their lives. What I think is that at least the film showed part of what the true Iraqi life was, and what it was for four musicians struggling to reach their goal, just to do what they were all passionate about. It's not an easy movie to watch, but at least you have to see it once to understand that people there are not kidding around, they are literally digging their own way. So I believe that this movie had a lot of points describing that.

BRIAN: We tried to get the band into Berlin for the International Film Festival there. That's when we realized that the Saddam-era passports were a serious problem. The people at the Berlin International Film Festival were unbelievably helpful. This woman, Elá Gurmen, was Turkish and very enthusiastic about getting them in. They were all very upset when they didn't make it. This was when we started to realize—Berlin was in February—that we needed to do something. I don't want to get philosophical, but it's hard to wrap your head around the fact that if you don't do something, nothing happens at all. And if we don't do something, these guys are fucked. And it's a tough realization, especially when we all just love to downplay the importance of anything we do, even if it is actually important. So it was kind of weird to put yourself in the mind-set; that was what really got tough.

When we were in Berlin, that was the time Suroosh was communicating with someone else on this, being like, "Actually, yeah, we need to really do something."

SUROOSH: We did some research, the guys did some research, and found that Turkey was the only place you could fly to as an Iraqi without a visa. It all started around the time of the Toronto festival. We put together the website, put the PayPal account on it, started asking for donations, and raised enough money, bought the tickets, and got them out.

MARWAN: The rules said that whoever comes to Turkey from Iraq needed $2,000 on them so they knew you would invest it in tourism. So we told Suroosh that we needed $2,000 each for six people, including Firas's wife and son. So he set up that donation through *Vice*.

Even for *Vice* that was a lot of money, but I remember in four days Suroosh called and laughed and said, "Do you know how much we collected?"

I said, "How much?"

He said, "Ten thousand dollars."

"You are joking!"

He said, "No, people from all over the world were giving money."

Then the level started rising again, up to $17,000. We were

amazed. It was a huge amount of money. I don't know if we under-estimated ourselves and the band thing, being caught up in the bu-reaucracy, or if we just got lucky. Either way, people all around the world made a really powerful statement by donating.

MONICA: It's definitely been an interesting process, because you usually just make a film and in the end, you're friendly with your subjects but it's usually not so intimate as this has been. But it feels like, "What are you going to do?" You're doing a film about refugees, you're documenting their struggle, and at a certain point, you actually have the ability to help get them out of that. It's common for a docu-mentary to take years, and I think people do tend to get close to their subjects at times, but we never set out to help them to the extent that we did. It all just happened very organically and there was no motivation for anything except, "Shit, we can help these people. It's not that difficult for us." Why not help them if we can do it?

BERNARDO: The first time I actually met them was in Turkey. Firas grabbed the camera from me . . . We were on the train from eastern Istanbul, and he asked me, "What is it about us that's so interesting?" They started interviewing me and Suroosh. What I thought was, I had been working for two years on Iraq-related projects, a lot of veterans and people who have lost people in the war. I felt I was pretty involved but I had never seen Iraqis that I could relate to. All of a sudden there was this footage of kids my age and who look like they could be my friends. I had bands of my own when I was in high school.

FIRAS: When we got to Turkey, the world started paying more atten-tion. I mean, yeah, the world was already paying attention since the band started, but after the war and the film came out, things were getting bigger and bigger and bigger and bigger. You don't know where you're gonna end up, you just turn around and follow the flow.

And then Middle Eastern media starts paying attention, and then also the Iraqi media starts paying attention. So metalheads all over the world know that there's a band from Iraq, and here we are and we still exist. Because even people in Iraq, they thought we vanished, we got killed, we left the country, we broke up, we quit the band. So it's just good for the people who care to know.

And that has us feeling kind of worried about our families, relatives who live there, that they might get hurt just because we did that. Let's wish for the better.

Because we got all this attention, we started to turn into sort of like puppets—some way or another someone will turn the table around and just put you to serve some political reasons, or articles for politics bullshit. But as we say always, and I mean all of us, "We don't give a fuck about politics." So hopefully people will get it now. We are doing this first of all for ourselves, second of all for our country, and that's it. As a country I'm saying people, metalheads, audience. I'm not talking politically, I'm talking on a people level because I'm just a person. I'm not a politician, I'm not an analyst.

MONICA: I don't think politics were ever something that was consciously in our minds as we were making it. We were just documenting this real-life happenstance, and we weren't trying to comment either way. Is it political because they want to get out of there? It's stronger without the politics. You can make up your own mind about what's right and what's wrong based on what they see. They're just a band and it just so happens that they were born in Iraq.

FIRST TIME THE BAND
SEES SNOW, TAKSIM
SQUARE, ISTANBUL, 2008.
PHOTO BY AHMET POLAT.

10

FOR WHOM THE BELL TOLLS

MARWAN: I had been in Syria for a year and a half when we left for Istanbul.

When we left Syria, we all went to the airport together. *Vice* got us the tickets after we decided we wanted to go there. We all agreed that Turkey would be the only place to get refugee status.

We had tried to go to Canada, and we went to the embassy twice but got rejected—apparently we did not "satisfy" them. I said, "How can I satisfy you?" I was harassing the embassy employee because she was kind of mean to us. I don't feel like I am talking to a living being when there is a window between us—I feel like I am talking to "authority" or something—so I was trying to make jokes, the guys were laughing. I hate it when people treat us like objects and files.

We got rejected twice.

FAISAL: Turkey was a big place to discover. It was nice for someone who's rich, someone who's got business there, someone traveling and having fun with his family, but we had a different road to take. We were refugees.

It was kinda similar to our culture, so we had an easy time mixing with the people over there, but it was still hard for us because of the language and the money we had to spend to stay alive.

Plus, we never knew how long we would be there for. We didn't know whether we could stay and begin our lives again or have to move on somewhere else. It was a constant feeling of unease.

MARWAN: I remember we said good-bye to everyone and went to Tony's house. His mum was crying, asking me to take care of him. I said to her, "We aren't going off to war." Little did I know.

Then we got in the car, got the guys, and left for the airport. And every time we got through another bit of the airport there was another guy missing. By the time we reached the plane it was only me and Faisal.

The reason? We didn't satisfy immigration. There were some problems with some of the guys' paperwork. Nothing was easy for us. So me and Faisal were at the final exit to the plane and we were holding the door open. Faisal had his hand on the door and I was half in, half out. And I said to Faisal, "What do you think?"

He said, "Should we go to Turkey or stay?"

I said, "Where are the guys? Let's head back!"

We changed our minds and got off the plane. There was a certain rule at the airport that said that because of that, we had to be held for an hour, due to security measures.

It turns out that Tony had had a problem with his passport picture and Firas's son had a problem with the name on his. And we went back all tired and disappointed. We bought some kebabs as consolation. We slept on our bags as we had given the keys to our basements to the owners. We slept in one basement together. Then a week later, after some help from *Vice*, we tried to get out again. This time we were frightened and the *Vice* guys were really frustrated.

We decided to all go alone so that if one of us got stopped it would not cause trouble for the others and waste money. And we all got past the checkpoints! Then we got to Jordan and from there to Turkey. And after that, for the first twenty days everything was on hold . . . we felt really paranoid. We were calling *Vice* all the time—we didn't know the place or the language.

We rented a place and got out of the hotel we first stayed in— while we were at the hotel, somebody jacked $1,000 off me. When I woke up, the door was open and I saw Tony pointing at the exit. They took my wallet. Bad luck. Around about that time MTV contacted us, but actually our first interview was with the BBC. Then people started knowing about us, the Turkish media got frenzied about us as they had this big peace movement. They set up concerts for us, and we thought, "Okay, finally!"

Then Suroosh and Bernardo and John came over, and this is where Cengiz came into the picture. He was our Turkish punk friend—he is thirty-seven or something, but he is cool and eccentric. He has also been influenced a lot by Western culture. Plus, he was real helpful, and suddenly he was our man on the ground and *Vice*'s man, too.

CENGIZ TANC (PRODUCER, *HEAVY METAL IN ISTANBUL*): I'd been following their story for a while. It had been on VBS for a year, I think, and they sent out a message saying they were looking for funds. I had no money but I thought I could help them if they came to Turkey. They were saying they needed to get out of Iraq, to some

HANGING OUT WITH MEMBERS OF THE RED WOLVES MOTORCYCLE GANG
AFTER A SHOW, KEMANCI CLUB, ISTANBUL, 2007.

interim place before they got asylum in the First World. I thought
Turkey would be perfect. I sort of have contacts here and am settled
in . . . my dad works for the foreign ministry, so we have government
contacts. I thought if they came, we could set them up with maybe a
job in Istanbul. Turkey is a good midway point, a stepping-stone.

The first time I met Firas and Faisal, we had a lot of fun. We were
in one of the bars they sort of discovered while here, a bar I'd never
been to before, in kind of a busy area, that was a heavy metal place.
That's when it all clicked. I didn't meet Marwan that night because
he had other plans and Tony's a homebody anyway. Eventually it
became more Marwan and I hanging out.

FAISAL: We finally played some shows in Turkey. At one of them, a bunch of biker guys showed up. Suroosh said to Ahmet, the photographer, that he wanted to take photos with the bikers. I was like, "Dude, this is impossible. These guys look aggressive, so I don't want to mess with them." But actually it just turned out that he said nice words to them. The bikers were interested in *Vice* and heavy metal. And we were happy with that, just to see others familiar with the metal scene. The guys were so welcoming, so polite with us. They were talking and laughing with us and we were being more social.

JOHN MARTIN (ASSOCIATE PUBLISHER, *VICE* MAGAZINE): They played a show at this place called Komanci Club, which was not a bad vibe for a club; the setup was great and it was obviously set up by an aging Scandinavian rock dude who partied with Mötley Crüe on tour in '88 and then moved to Turkey and started a club. It was that weird older dude, kinda gothy, hard rock, skulls vibe. He was definitely glam rock-y, Tommy Lee. His name was Nikki Wilde.

At the show they got asked for an encore, but they had played so few shows they weren't ready. People were psyched and they ripped through all their songs. At the end, everyone was screaming for an encore, and they were like, "Oh shit, we don't have any more songs! Okay, we're gonna play 'Gardens of Stone' one more time!" At the end of their show, which was probably around eleven or something, Firas just goes, "Okay, now everyone go home," and Nikki was in the DJ booth and you saw him look all pissed off, and he just intoned in this voice of God, "No. *You* go home."

FIRAS: The first show in Turkey was really great, other than the media attention. I hated it. Reporters from all over the world, standing in line, and you tell them the same story over and over. Some of them didn't have anything to ask us. They'd come in, "Hello, hello, this and that," and we'd just tell them a story and they'd pick up whatever

ACRASSICAUDA MEETS TESTAMENT, ISTANBUL, 2008.

they wanted to, because we just got tired of it. If the story was about our music, then it'd be fine, but it was all about us being refugees. We are not a freak show.

MARWAN: I liked Turkey for a while. We met the band Testament there when they were playing in Istanbul. Tony had a DVD of them performing in England and we were watching it, saying how cool they are, and *Vice* called and said they wanted to meet us. Unbelievable. They gave us Alex Skolnick's number and said he was expecting our call. We were like high school kids—"Shall we call him now? Shall we?"—and eventually I called. Tony was giggling, and I said, "Hello, is this Mr. Alex?" And he was like, "Yeah! Who is this?"

"It's Marwan!"

"Marwan who?"

"Marwan from Acrassicauda."

"Oh great. You guys have got to come to the concert."

And so we did.

It was the first real concert any of us had gone to see. We were doing the devil horns and stuff. We had tried to see a band before but it had never happened. Anyway, they performed, it was fantastic, and the one thing that was most exciting for me was that Paul Bostaph, who used to play in Slayer, was in the band. Paul was my idol since ages ago, so it was like a double joy for me. We headbanged our asses off and started a mosh pit. I lost my voice, we took our shirts off, I hurt my eye.

After the show, as we walked past the fence, the band was leaving, and all these people were trying to get to them and talk to them. I shouted at Alex, and he let me in through the fence to meet the band. He had been looking through the crowd for us. All these kids tried to swarm in, but they got me in okay and then the rest of the guys.

They were amazing. They were so interested in us, and seemed to know all about us. I even became friends with Paul Bostaph. We now email a lot. He gave me tips on drumming, and he was a really down-to-earth guy. I am looking forward to seeing him again.

FIRAS: When we met Testament, it was awesome and I couldn't believe it. Meeting one of our idols, one of the bands that we dreamed we'd be like someday, was amazing. I was like, "So do you guys have private jets? Do you have limousines?" And they thought that was funny but I honestly thought they might have had those things.

ALEX SKOLNICK (TESTAMENT): I learned that the band had temporarily found refuge in Istanbul. As it turned out, Testament had just been booked for Turkey's annual Uni-Rock festival, to take place in Istanbul the following June. This presented the perfect opportunity to invite Acrassicauda to our show. I put in the word to

Vice and immediately heard back that the guys would like nothing more than to attend our show, adding that Marwan could not stop saying, "It's fucking Testament!"

After our set that night, I felt I was meeting five long-lost friends: Firas, Faisal, Tony, Marwan, and their buddy. They couldn't wait for me to introduce them to the rest of Testament, who hadn't seen the film yet but looked forward to meeting the Iraqi guys I'd told them about. Acrassicauda, who had seemed so tense and jaded in the film, were now like kids in a candy store, having just seen their first-ever Western metal concert (after all, how many tours stop in Iraq?) and going backstage to meet one of their favorite bands.

Right away I felt like I knew these guys. They seemed just like any other cool metal guys from other countries. They spoke pretty good English (much of it learned from metal lyrics). They used the F-word a lot. They wore black T-shirts with logos of their favorite bands. They had a great sense of humor (despite all they were going through) and loved metal. They wanted the same things most of us want, to be able to pursue our dreams and have a good time doing it. But for them, like anyone else from Iraq, it hasn't been so easy.

MARWAN: Meeting Testament and the concert was fun, but soon enough we started to feel like refugees again. The official meaning of "refugee" means I am an asylum seeker, and I need to find a safe country that I can live in that accepts asylum seekers. It meant that I can't go back to my country for a certain reason, and that reason is that it wasn't safe.

Eventually, it was decided on all sides that it was time to go to America. Before we could get there, what we needed to do was go through the process of getting resettled in different satellite cities, because you can't be in Istanbul, it's overpopulated, and we couldn't see that. A lot of people just leave their settlement places and come back to Istanbul.

THE BAND RECEIVES SOME GIFTS FROM CONVERSE, ISTANBUL, 2008.

They told us that this time, if we wanted to get out and go to a new country, we had to do it by the book. So we were each resettled in a different place.

First, Tony was resettled about five hours away from Istanbul and the last person was Faisal. It was really frustrating. All the time we were waiting to see if we would be accepted into America.

JOHN: I originally got involved because Converse didn't have an ad campaign and so their agency requested that every magazine bring a "create their own" campaign that was all about, you know, fighting the status quo. So I just pitched them on this idea of doing a campaign and some online video around Acrassicauda, because these guys fled their homeland and everything, and are now living life as a band on

THE BAND WALKS WITH SUROOSH TO THEIR PRACTICE SPACE IN ISTANBUL DURING THE SHOOTING OF *HEAVY METAL IN ISTANBUL*, 2008. PHOTO BY AHMET POLAT.

the run. And so they actually bit, and they gave us some money to do it. So me, Suroosh, and Bernardo, and a big, big bag of Converse shoes and clothes for the guys and their friends, went to Istanbul and met up with Cengiz, the fixer, who's a great dude, and met up with the guys and brought guitars and instruments for everyone except Marwan. It's hard to bring drums on a plane. And so we started filming and stayed in Istanbul for five days.

It's funny, because they kind of stick out, and I hadn't met them yet but had seen the movie at that point. We literally saw them coming. There's this avenue in Turkey which is the pedestrian mall and that's where our hotel was. It's a massive teeming sea of humanity, very European, very cool. And we're waiting for them, just looking back and forth, kind of disoriented, because we don't know where they're coming from, and immediately you can tell who they are because they're all in black, wallet chains, black hats, black leather jackets, hair that's growing out a little bit and goatees, and so they just look different. Oh, and they had guitars on their backs, too. Everyone was cool at first, there was like a definite getting-to-know-you period, but we went out to dinner that first day and once the ice was broken they were just your typical twenty-something-year-old dudes, whether they're in Iraq or Iowa. They like to fuck around, interacting as buddies and breaking balls. They rip on each other, and once you figure out the dynamics that they all rip on each other with, then you just jump right into that.

It was really cold when we were there because it was the middle of winter, and Istanbul is cold, but Ankara is *really* cold. It's like going from New York City to Montréal. And so we had brought them all the shoes and hooded sweatshirts and T-shirts and everything, and it makes sense that they gravitated toward the black T-shirts and the hoodies. The shoes, not so much. "It's cold. It's winter now." And I'm saying, "What's the big deal? I wear Converse in winter." They were actually telling jokes like, "Wow, when we lived in Syria, these were the cool shoes that you just couldn't get, they were just

ON THE TRAIN TO THE UNITED NATIONS HIGH COMMISSION OF REFUGEES,
ANKARA, 2008. PHOTOS BY AHMET POLAT.

unavailable, and it's so weird that you guys are bringing these boxes of shoes now."

We took the night train to Ankara and we took photos just drinking beers on the train, band hijinx, the little kid with the beer cans, and we got some great photos in there. It was all really natural. The crux of the whole journey was, "We are going to the United Nations High Commissioner of Refugees [UNHCR] to get their legal status either confirmed or denied. This is going to have a happy ending or a sad ending." The guys don't accept the bureaucracy level of what they're going through—they find it very demoralizing. That was one thing that Bernardo and I talked to them about: "Yes, you do have to break through a lot of red tape, but as long as something is happening and you're not just in a waiting game, that means things are happening, you're getting one step closer. It's just you're gonna have a lot of steps to go through."

So we get off the train in the morning and we're late and everyone just jumps into cabs, all bleary-eyed and unshowered, cameras rolling, "Take us to the UN!" It is cold as fuck. We pull up and you wouldn't think this was the United Nations—it just looked like a pretty nondescript residential road going up a hill with apartment buildings on it, except there was a security gate and a guard.

The guys got in, but media couldn't. Cengiz ended up talking to a succession of people at the gate, I think he told them that we were American media, and Western media showing up is a big deal. We got an interview with this guy, Eduardo Yrzebal, who is the second in command there, and he sat down with us for an hour, and we're these scraggly dudes with cameras. He was very familiar with the case, because these guys were in their edition of *Rolling Stone* that was out on stands while we were there, and they'd been on TV. He didn't want to say he thought they'd get out, but he spelled it out for us: "This is what happens to refugees, these are the steps they have to go through, your guys are well known."

Then he actually took us down to the waiting room, where they hold all the refugees. It was like a cross between a doctor's office waiting room and a prison visitor's room. Yeah, there's little chairs and coloring books for kids, but there's *also* bars on the door and it's in a basement. So we walked in there and Ahmet Polat is with us and a couple of the guys are hanging out and some others are conducting their interview. The whole place is filled with what we can only assume are Sudanese and Somali refugees. It was a grim scene—people who have had humanity fail them.

Ahmet stayed and the rest of us went back out and froze our asses off. We went to get tea—they love drinking chai in Turkey. Ahmet comes out a little while later: "I just got so many pictures, it's great." Eventually they all come out, hours later. We then held court in a local restaurant for a good four hours, ordered everything on the menu, but it was great. The pictures that came out are amazing: the guys sitting there, looking distraught, and you can see the other faces behind them, and you realize, yeah, they're one cool story, but there are so many others.

The guys went in and were separated, even though their case was being handled pretty much as one. So they all go and have separate interviews, where they have to explain their lives, I guess, and why they don't want to go back to Iraq, and so on. It took all day.

They were assigned to a town called Sivas, which means they had to leave Istanbul and go to this satellite city. Sivas has special significance because it was known for the Sivas Massacre, and it's about eight hours away from Ankara. That was the satellite city they were supposed to go to, and they figured they could live in Istanbul and do this crazy commute once a week. The Sivas Massacre occurred due to a hotbed of fundamentalism—in '93, there were some intellectuals that were firebombed, and about thirty people died. It's a pretty well–known day of infamy in Turkish history, and the band already knew that the western Turkish area is full of fundamentalism. And they had received death threats, and they were saying, "Now that we're known, we don't want to put ourselves or our families in jeopardy."

When we went to Ankara, they officially became refugees. The country knew they were there. They weren't gonna get picked up by the police or anything. Turkey is a Western country. It's not as sketchy as a lot of other places. You're not gonna get picked up unless you're fighting in the street or you're actually doing something wrong.

And when we got back to Istanbul, there were these cool posters all over that one main street where they just said in a yellow font "Sivas '93," and there was this picture on the poster of this burning building. Was it for a play or a TV documentary or something? We walk by and they're like, "Why Sivas?" And I point and say, "Oh, Sivas like *that*?" They looked at the poster and they go, "Holy shit, that's where we have to go?" And they didn't end up going, and that screwed them a little bit. They got reassigned, so they didn't end up going to Sivas, and I think that ruffled some feathers.

FIRAS: Even when we heard the words that we were approved to go to the United States it was a painful moment, both emotionally and mentally. Yeah, I may end up in the United States but I wasn't sure about my friends, or about what kind of life I'd be living there or how people would treat me there since I'm from Iraq. It was a lot of things I had to worry about, so many things.

It was the emotional pain of being far away from home, as far as I'd ever been. Even in Turkey I felt it was close, I could be back in Baghdad in a couple of hours at the most. But in the States, you would be half a world away. That just freaked us out.

CENGIZ: Tony and Firas were the first to leave Turkey to go to America. It was insane. It was that whole, "We're really excited to be getting to the airport," and I'm getting my own personal relief like, "Okay, I'm getting rid of half of them!" I love them and everything, but it's a constant back and forth of people getting in trouble and then I get in trouble because when they're suffering I feel responsible and they're my friends and it brings me down. So to see them go and see them finally succeed is like me succeeding as well. It was an immense relief. We get to the airport and there's a lot of waiting and uncertainty, but you never know what's going to happen or what's going to go wrong. And, of course, there were too many people there and they overbooked the flight so they didn't fly out in the morning and they were told, "You have to come back tomorrow night," or something like that.

They had to get a special car because there was so much baggage and they had already said good-bye to everyone, and then they didn't leave and had to go back home, and so I had to take the kid and the wife back and Firas and Tony stayed the night at the airport. We hardly got any sleep, but I woke up because Firas called me at ten in the morning and said, "They might be flying us out earlier," and all I thought was, Whew, thank God.

So I picked up the kid and the wife and shot over to the airport and everything seemed to be going well, but we were late and Firas was calling me on the way there, yelling, "Where are you? Where are you?"

The guy from the International Organization for Migration was harassing Firas: "Where are they? Where are they? Because if they're not here in two minutes, then we're not going to be able to check you in," and it was that close but it worked out. That's when I knew, when I saw them go through passport control. "Woo-hoo! They're going! They're off."

I think we were talking about doughnuts, for some reason. I was saying, "You guys are gonna love doughnuts," and I kind of explained what they were, and the guys loved it. So I texted Brian telling him he should have doughnuts waiting for them.

FAISAL: I had problems with my satellite city, Kastamonu, in the north of Turkey. The government was very strict and said I couldn't leave there until I got the all-clear to go to America, but I didn't have money to stay there. So what? They were gonna leave me staying in the street or something? They said, "Don't worry, we're gonna find you some Iraqi folks, they're refugees, too, you can sleep with them."

Okay, so they were Iraqis from my home country, but I can't trust strangers, no matter where they're from. So I kept searching around the whole city for a cheap motel. I found one for about five dollars a day. You share the toilets—it's like a hostel.

But it was clean, at least, and I got my own privacy and my own door I could lock. I stayed there for about a week and then came back to Istanbul, which I wasn't supposed to do. But it was the Bayram holiday, and Kastamonu was basically closed for ten days, and all I was doing there was wasting money on the motel. And one of the police officers from Kastamonu called me, while I was in Istanbul, three days before the end of Bayram, and he told me, "Where are you? Come get your exit letter."

I lied and said, "I'm actually sick and not staying in the same hotel."

THE BAND AT THEIR HOME IN ISTANBUL, 2008. PHOTO BY AHMET POLAT.

And right away he said, "You're lying to me, you're not in the city. You're back in Istanbul, right?"

I said, "No, no, no, I'm in the city, but I don't know where I am. I'm sitting in some friend's house."

"Okay, tell me the address."

"I'm sick. I can't leave yet."

Believe me, I'm a terrible liar.

So, he told me, "Okay, quit bullshitting me. Remember this—your exit letter will be delayed for who knows how long. Just stop it."

He hung up on me, and then I sat there, crushed. I mean, I only had a few days left to leave the country and go to America and all I could think was, What the hell have I done?

CENGIZ: When Firas was going to the airport, there was a big mess with the tickets not working, but Faisal's problem was a lot more serious.

He was basically screwed because it was two days before his flight and if he couldn't get his exit papers now, he probably wouldn't make it. The way this cop talked to him, he was going to hand him over for not being in the city when he called, and if you get busted on an infraction like that, it's all over. Usually people deal with it by going to the police they know and bribes are paid.

Faisal and I were sitting in IKEA with my girlfriend. We went to the bus station to try to get him back to the satellite city as fast as we could get him back, but the buses had already left, and the next one was too late.

So we're in IKEA eating Swedish meatballs. At one point he said, "I'm really frightened, I'm really scared." And that was as raw as it could get. That's when I was like, "I gotta deal with this, we have to get an answer." We were just in limbo, and had no strategy. Should we call the guy and tell the truth? Or get him back there so he could show up at the police station the next morning? So we decided to tell the truth, and I went outside and I called the cop, and I was supernervous, too.

I was like, "Man, if I fuck this up, he goes back to Iraq."

So I called the cop and said, "It's kind of my fault that this happened. He had no money." And the guy was like, "Why did he lie?"

"He's just a kid, he was scared, but he's a good guy. He feels really bad."

Because I was a Turk, it calmed him down.

I said, "Please take care of him," and he said he would. I told him, "If you ever come to Istanbul, I'll take care of you," so we worked it out.

FAISAL: Cengiz showed up and he said, "You gotta take the first bus you're gonna get and you're going to get your ass over there and just apologize to him, and I talked to him and explained and gave him all the details that I could give him, and I told him that you didn't mean it: 'He was just scared, he was out of money. I told him to come to my place. If you want to blame somebody, blame it on me.'"

It was such a good gesture from him. I owe him and I'm never going to forget him.

He kept reminding me, "Be cool with it. Don't worry, you're gonna come back." I did what he said—I got on the first bus I could get, I went to the city, waited until the police station opened. I told the cop, "I'm sorry, I didn't have a choice." He kept telling me, "Why did you lie? Why didn't you tell me?" And I said, "You didn't give me any chance." At this moment he said, "Okay, this is your exit letter. Sign here and your plane is at one o'clock, so you have to be at the airport at about eight to go on with the process with the bag searching and all that." I said, "Okay, no problem. Thank you."

I didn't even get my hands on the letter when the ICMC [International Catholic Migration Commission] called me. "Faisal?" I was like, "Yeah! I know I'm flying tomorrow! Yeahhhh!" And they said, "Actually, your flight's been extended and we had to put you on another date because your medical checks already expired."

So at that moment, I was trying to grab the exit letter but I didn't have the chance to touch it.

I was numb: "Say what? Say again? Please. Say again. Tell me you're kidding me. Please tell me you're kidding me. I'm begging you."

She was like, "No. I'm sorry to be the person to give you the bad news, but it just happened."

I was crushed again. Totally out of control, crying. I told her, "Please, I'll do the examination. What do you need from me? I'll go as soon as I reach the city." I had already booked the bus ticket and had about fifteen minutes to head to the big city. And she gives me that news.

Fuck it. I had to risk it. I asked the police officer, "What if my flight is extended for about two or three more days? What's gonna happen?" He said, "No, you're gonna have to get back in the city and register with the authority because here it says the fifteenth of

December, and if you're gonna go to the airport with that date that's already been approved, they're not going to allow you to get out." I get back on the phone, and the girl from the ICRC says: "I talked to the manager and I begged him that it was my responsibility to let you come, but he said no way because the health examination is gonna take four to five hours, you won't make the flight. And the only time the hospital will open is eight or eight thirty in the morning, so you won't be able to fly out on time." I said, "I don't know what do, but seriously, do something. I'm not blaming you or anyone else, but please find me an answer. I don't have anything left, not a penny in my pockets, so please. I spent my last money on the bus ticket, so I'm heading to Istanbul and from there I'm gonna go to the airport. Tell me what to do."

She was actually sympathizing with me a lot, saying, "I'm really sorry I have to give you this news. I hate my job for doing this!"

I thought I was going to pass out any minute, just because of all these things coming toward me emotionally. I was heading to the city, so I had to spend three or fours hours on the bus, just destroyed. I had to close my phone until we got to a rest area, so this woman called me when I got there and told me, "You got another flight on the seventeenth." I thought about it, "The seventeenth, that means two days." It was like noon at that point, so what the hell was I gonna do? I'm already on the bus to Istanbul, till ten o'clock at night, I'm not gonna do anything tonight, I have to do all the exams the next morning. At seven thirty I would head to the hospital, take the exams for four or five hours, that means like eleven thirty. After that, I would head to the bus office and reserve the twelve o'clock bus, head back to Kastamonu, another ten hours, and I thought, I'm not gonna make it. I thought it was going to take two or three hours signing and all that stuff at the police station. I called Cengiz as soon as possible, and I told him, "Dude, what should I do? The police officer says I have to go back to the city to extend my exit letter."

Cengiz couldn't do anything, because this is a law matter. I guess, yeah, if I'm a police officer at the airport and I saw somebody's heading somewhere after the date on the exit letter, that will be a big trouble for him and for me. So I had to go through all this again and again for three or four more hours, until I reached Istanbul.

Then I checked my phone and I had a message from Cengiz that said, "Hey, buddy, you won't have to go to the satellite city."

And I was screaming and so happy and jumping in the bus station. I was so excited, I didn't believe it.

So the next day I had to go to the hospital first thing, like at seven thirty or eight, and make my examination. I had nothing else. When I went the next morning, I went to the ICMC and asked for the girl who had called me. They told me, "Why?" "I just want to speak to her in person." When she showed up, "Are you Faisal? I'm so sorry!" I told her, "Thank you," and I hugged her. It was a really touching moment because I was on the edge of drowning, on the verge of losing everything, and I kept saying, "Seriously, thank you."

MARWAN: With the guys gone, I was left all alone in Turkey. Staying in hotel rooms was nasty, feeling alone and left behind. There was no way to keep my spirits up. We used to have the band but now there was nothing, even my friends were gone. I just sat at home watching TV or sleeping and feeling frustrated. I had to ask to sleep on people's couches and stuff. Firas's brother and sister-in-law let me stay for a while, but it was really hard for me having no place or privacy. But people were very kind to me. I was carrying my life with me for almost three months, like a Gypsy. I had to give up the house, I couldn't pay for it alone once the others were resettled. My relationships didn't go well, but a lot of people helped me and I didn't expect it. I owe them.

When I got my visa papers it was a relief: "Finally. I am leaving."

I was meant to be going with Faisal, and then they called me and denied me. It was a devastating moment. I aged ten years. I had just gotten my exit papers, they were in my hand, and they were saying, "Yeah, we are sorry."

The American embassy told the UNHCR to tell me my visa had been denied and my flight had been canceled—they didn't even explain why.

I did not know whether to laugh or cry. I had just had it in my brain that I was leaving. And it was taken away. And what is worse is that you don't feel like they owe you anything, they are doing *you* a favor, so whatever they decide is okay. Humans always plan ten steps ahead, which is a mistake, because it only takes one person's decision to tear it all down.

I was in purgatory, man. I didn't know what to do. The guys had left by the New Year, and I started getting used to the idea that I may never get my visa; I was resigned to that.

I told myself to get used to the idea that the guys may get a new drummer. What I had worked on for years, the band, was over. My friends were telling me it was okay, and I was saying, "Yeah, but it's eight years of work, gone."

They were like, "You should be optimistic."

I said, "Tell me why? What should give me hope? What can I hold in my hands that should make me optimistic?"

It was rough.

New Year's came. I was hoping to spend it with my friends but then I couldn't take it anymore, it was torture, I couldn't sleep. Then I was like, "Fuck it, I tried my best." Then there was the going back and forth to the satellite city dozens of times. It was five or six hours away and I did it just to save money. It drained me.

I became used to it, what more could I have done?

I said to myself, "You know what, Marwan? If you go back to Iraq, it's not a nightmare, it'll be okay."

I created this mind state where it was okay to go back. That's

when I settled down a bit, I started sleeping a bit. The nightmares stopped.

I just wanted to be with my band, but it seemed unlikely, since they got their visas, it seemed like a dead end. I even looked into it, I asked the police, and they said I was right, I should ask to end my refugee status and get papers to go back to Iraq. I spoke to my family about it. I was resigned to it. My dream was thousands of miles away.

I started going out, not caring about anything. I was going with the flow. This isn't the way I am but this is the way I had to be, because for a second, I didn't see the light at the end of the tunnel, just a bunch of fat bellies on desks telling me what to do.

I stopped caring about anything. I loosened up a bit. And I lost my desire to go out.

It was like when someone gives you a piece of bread when you are really hungry, then snatches it away. You lose your desire and all you have is anger. Then after the anger goes, all you have left to lose is the spirit. And that was where I was. I was totally unbothered. I used to sleep like fourteen hours a day, wake up, and feel tired. People talked to me and I was like, "Whatever." Suroosh used to call, or Brian, and I would ask them questions and get frustrated. They tried to keep my spirits up. I think the situation affected both sides badly, since it lasted a month and a half.

You lose your serenity and you don't have any sanctuary. Suicide? I had thought about it. It might be a solution that knocks on your door in moments of desperation, but if you think about it, really, it's not. It is the moment when your problems defeat you. But here is a place where there is no honor in taking your life. Being brave is about being able to *face* your life.

MARWAN, PRACTICE
SPACE, ISTANBUL, 2008.
PHOTO BY AHMET POLAT.

**MARWAN IS INTERVIEWED AS HE ARRIVES
IN THE U.S., NEWARK AIRPORT, JANUARY 2009.**

11

...AND JUSTICE FOR ALL

BRIAN: The International Refugee Committee [IRC] is a nongovernmental organization that helped us get all the guys over together, among a ton of other organizations and people who helped us. Within like a week of contacting them, this was the blinding speed of meetings coordinating press strategy, finding out what *Vice* could do and what they could do. Because most refugees come here knowing no one, knowing no English, having never been to a city, so it's not even like New York is daunting, the concept of public transportation and indoor plumbing is daunting.

FAISAL ARRIVES IN THE U.S., JFK AIRPORT, DECEMBER 2009.
PHOTOS BY LISA WHITEMAN.

Emily Holland became our person at the IRC. So they were say-ing, "You guys orient them and we'll do this," and I actually signed a document making me the anchor, which I think makes me a relative of theirs?

EMILY HOLLAND (SENIOR SPECIAL PROJECTS OFFICER, IRC): At that time, the band members had each been given refugee status by the UN refugee agency, UNHCR, but their individual cases had been allocated to different resettlement agencies in different U.S. cities.

KELLY AGNEW-BARAJAS (REGIONAL DIRECTOR, IRC): That would have looked like one going to Tennessee, one going to another agency in California, and they would have been far from each other.

EMILY: These guys aren't a traditional family, but in times of war they were everything to each other. So this friend of the IRC asked if we could help, and we said we'd do our best. We were able to intervene and resettle all four band members. We worked with *Vice* to keep the band together.

KELLY: The bureaucracy involved in making a change like that, especially a request for nonfamily members, is quite a big hurdle. And then on top of that, make sure they all come to New York rather than one in San Jose and one in Dallas. Brian became the anchor, or the sponsor.

EMILY: It involved many phone calls, in-person meetings, and strategizing. There were definitely days when I would speak more with Suroosh and Brian than my colleagues next door. We fought hard.

KELLY: They were in Turkey at the time, and Brian was on the phone with them every day, just dealing with the exit visas, which is a very common problem in Turkey. A lot of the refugees we're getting from Iraq are either from Jordan or Syria, so they don't experience that same type of bureaucracy, the problems of getting these exit visas, the security checks—that's a problem that's endemic for all refugees post-9/11, particularly with Iraqi refugees—name checks and FBI checks. It is a draconian system of security checks.

EMILY: Being at the airport when Firas and Tony arrived was an extremely moving experience. Suroosh, Brian, Monica, and I were there, doing the typical stakeout. It can take several hours for a newly arrived refugee to clear Customs. We were waiting and waiting, and the hours just ticked by, and there's no cellphone reception in the JFK arrivals terminal. We made coffee runs to try and stay awake, but each second you were gone, you worried you were going to miss

Firas and Tony's entrance. It was intense . . . and then finally, when the guys walked through, it was just . . . it was beautiful.

MONICA: The first time I met any of the guys was when we picked up Firas and Tony at the airport, in September of 2008. We went to the airport and we got there and we just waited for hours. We couldn't believe that they were still in Customs. We kind of missed them coming out. We're there holding the cameras up, waiting for hours, every time the door would open. Finally Suroosh goes outside for a cigarette, Brian's in the bathroom or something, everyone is all scattered, and all of a sudden they come through and we're all scrambling.

BRIAN: We're sitting there and it's getting extremely late and then Emily says, "There is a chance . . . sometimes they don't get through." And we're like, "Motherfucker." So during the cumulative minute and a quarter out of the seven hours waiting that Suroosh actually left the area, they walk out. I was finally stretching and turned the camera off to standby. And I see them and I'm trying to be all nonchalant because I know they don't know what I look like, and there's no one there that they would see. And then I can't remember exactly what happened, but running and screaming, just really happy and it's great and everyone's really excited, and then there's this lull, and then Suroosh references me, and they're like, "Where *is* fucking Brian?" And I'm standing there in front of them and they're like, "No fucking way." And they pick me up and I almost drop the camera, and they were shouting, "I thought you were like a fat bald lawyer or something!" and it was great.

So we waste a little time there and finally: "All right, let's go before they fucking change their minds or something." We stopped at a convenience store and that was when me and Firas first started talking and he starts getting really relaxed and making jokes. And then we try to figure out on our iPhones where we can eat, because at this point not only are we tired because most of us didn't eat or sleep, but we were experiencing the whole adrenaline comedown: "Okay, I don't have to worry about something for the first time in like fucking forever. There's a diner right there, let's go there." It was called the Vegas Diner. And we order like ten cheeseburgers. They checked out my iPod and made fun of me because I had only three songs by Metallica. Then we took them home—the apartment was clean, nice, big, full of toiletries, even had food.

FIRAS: After meeting the *Vice* guys and Emily at the airport we drove around a little bit, kind of—you know, just going all the way to New Jersey where we're staying. For a minute I felt like I was back in Baghdad but before the war, when everything was cool. We were crossing this bridge and we have the same in Baghdad but it's shorter, of course. I could see lights and stuff like that, people driving around nicely. But I still didn't know where I was going.

I didn't sleep for more than two days. I was worried and sad about so many things. It's a new experience, it's a new adventure. And also thinking: Am I gonna stay like this? Just touring all around the world? Is it gonna be the last stop for me? Just sit there? Settle there? I mean, all these things going through my mind, I don't know what to do.

BRIAN: After Firas and Tony got settled we had the first Thanksgiving. The IRC is now starting a tradition of the first Thanksgiving for refugees and people instrumental in refugee cases and everyone says thanks and it's just a nice little event. And there was supposed to be a big Hollywood star there and we didn't know who it was gonna be. So me and Suroosh are standing there and we couldn't get anyone on the phone. Firas came but we lost him at one point. Because everyone else is humanitarian this and secretary ambassador that, we literally felt like we snuck in. We're like, "What the fuck. If we don't come with our refugee they're gonna be like, 'We don't understand, who are you people?'" We felt so out of touch. Most of these people probably wear suits all the time. And Firas says, "Yo, that girl from *Star Wars* is here," and we're like, "Who?" And yeah, I actually met Natalie Portman by accident because I was just talking to Firas.

The Thanksgiving event was at an Ethan Allen store of all places, because the guy who owns Ethan Allen is very instrumental in the IRC. It was very weird, a very surreal night on all counts, but a lot of fun. They thought Firas (Tony wasn't there) was the sound guy, 'cause all the other refugees came in traditional garb and he came wearing a leather jacket and a Slayer T-shirt.

My mom is very, very family-oriented—"Let's bring people"—and she had mentioned Thanksgiving. I love her to death, but she tells me, "You should invite the band to Thanksgiving." I thought, You know what? I hate Thanksgiving, might as well at least have somebody enjoy it. I ended up having the best Thanksgiving *ever*. It was great because the band didn't know what the hell was going on, and my parents have a pretty big house so it was very cool for them to be there. It was me, Bernardo, Suroosh, Tony, and Firas just chillin' at my parents' house.

Budweiser-heavy and Marlboros and standing outside. They loved it. And my mom obviously made them both Tupperware containers full of food—they even went upstairs and played foosball in my old room.

When I heard that Marwan was good to go to come here, I was giddy. The Friday right before Kurban Bayram, which is a week-long holiday, a huge problem surfaced. So clearly for this week *nothing* is happening, and the Tuesday following that is when his flight would be. We had to find who was working that week to make this happen.

We decided not to publicize the first two dudes' arrival because we figured that would burn out the story. We were also told by the

IRC that that actually might harm the cases of the two dudes there because anytime . . . it was half in the hands of the UNHCR and half in the hands of the Turks, the legitimate Turks. So if they felt undue pressure, especially from the U.S., they'd turn around and say, "Oh yeah? Guess what? They're going nowhere. We have no need to do this." That was the problem; you've always got to think in these cases that it's not like a business thing, it's like they hold all the cards and can just say, "Fuck it! No one leaves ever again."

After Firas and Tony were here, the October 10 rumors came back. Marwan and Faisal started thinking about going back to Iraq. If they made a movie about this, that would be the scene in the preview when I'm begging them, "Guys, I swear to God, I know it's shitty for me to ask that you keep toughing this out." But *this* was my point of no return, I would say, because I absolutely promised something that I was not sure I could deliver.

I was telling them, "I swear to God, you're getting in. If it comes to me having to find some dude who will put a bag on your head and put you on a boat in a container ship coming over here, you are getting the fuck over here. I don't need to put too fine a point on it, but going back to Baghdad isn't exactly safe, especially for people who have had a Western movie made about them." And that would be our fault. It wouldn't hold up in a court of law, but it would definitely be our fault.

FAISAL: I remember the day I left Turkey to come to America. I fought with Marwan, because it's hard to leave and we're not good at saying good-bye. I headed to the airport alone, and I had to leave an acoustic guitar because it was too huge and I was over the weight. I had to go to the deposit office and leave it there and tell Marwan to grab it whenever he got the chance. Finally got on the plane. I was too excited. I kept thinking police would stop the plane. Everything went careful and slow, but right.

MARWAN ARRIVES IN THE U.S., NEWARK AIRPORT, JANUARY, 2009.
PHOTOS BY LISA WHITEMAN.

Hours later, I got off the plane and it was . . . we're above JFK Airport, and the guy who was sitting with me was also an Iraqi refugee, and we were like, "Okay, we're here in America. What else do you want? Another planet?" We couldn't believe it. There was New York and there was JFK. I was so excited that I was going to see the guys again, and I was really sad because Marwan didn't make it.

Going through Customs was easy. I thought it was going to be such a process and the security search all over again. All these stories I heard about the States' airports just kept driving me insane. "I'm gonna go through all that, I'm so exhausted." I waited for about half an hour, and they just took my stamp and my fingerprints and signature, checked my papers, told me to have a seat, and they finished with everything. The representative asked me, "Are you excited to see your guys and the States?"

"Oh yeah."

I went down the exit hall, and went in a lot of circles, until I reached the last door, and there, I saw Firas just running toward me. "Whoa!" He had way longer hair and he was screaming. I saw Suroosh and was like, "Hey!" When I first saw Brian, he was a shock actually. All of us kept hearing Brian's voice on the phone and he was like a serious guy—serious subjects, serious conversations. You can't hear a bad word from him, only in a few circumstances, I remember. So I thought Brian was going to be more mature, with gray hair or something, glasses and a suit. "How are you doing, Mr. Faisal?" And Suroosh says, "Hey, yeah, here's Brian."

"You're kidding me, right? What the hell, dude? I mean, seriously. You're Brian?!" I didn't know what to tell him—I thanked him. Just, "Thank you, for everything. You managed to get me here. I wouldn't forget anything. I'll never forget this favor."

EMILY: I arrived a couple of seconds after Faisal had exited Customs and will never forget him standing there in a black T-shirt with an enormous skull on the front. The first words I heard from his mouth, "Hi, honey, I'm home!" Then I turned to Firas and asked what this moment felt like. "All I want for Christmas is Marwan," he said, and smiled.

MARWAN: One day I was at a friend's house couch surfing in Turkey and I got a phone call out of the blue. It was a woman and she asked me to do my medical checks.

I said, "No, I'm not going to do them."

So she asked where I was. I told her I was at the resettlement place, but I was really in Istanbul, and she said, "Are you sure? So why don't you do your medical checks?" I said, "Well, my case is on hold and my visa got denied, and I don't know if I'll even be accepted or rejected because no one will explain what's going on."

Then she said, "Well, I have your file here, and I can see you have been given clearance."

I wasn't sure if I had heard her right. She said it like it was nothing. I asked her to repeat it. I was very clear.

I said, "Am I good to go?"

She said, "Yes, just get your medical checks and we can give you your departure date."

But this time I didn't jump up or anything, I just hung up and was like, "Okay." I was so excited after living in desperation and anticipation for six weeks.

I called Brian up and told him the news. He didn't believe me at first, it was too good to be true. I also said, "Don't tell the guys, though. I don't want to disappoint them again." Then I did my medical checks, and when I was coming down here I was happy and excited, but again they killed it with a long journey to the States. By the time I got here I was so tired I was numb.

But then I got here, and the first few weeks I actually felt homesick.

It's been good to see the guys again and have our second reunion, really good. It was a real relief. Finally I was here. We could do something together. All these days, being stuck in life's queue. Now it's time to get out of the queue and play some music.

FAISAL: I had a lot of moments with myself, thinking about whether I am going to make it or not, make it through this. And I never knew that it was going to be that complicated somehow. I knew it was going to be complicated in certain ways, like how you're going to use your identities, how you're going to surf New Yorkers' or Americans' ways. It's getting more obvious that I'm going a lot further than my own culture and starting a new one. It's just starting below the zero, it's not even the zero level. It hurts sometimes because each station you had in all these different trips—Baghdad, Syria, Turkey—each one of them had a special moment for each one of us. Now we're at this new level. We need to get up here or at least we reach the same level to see. It's more unexplained, unspeakable. We wanted to do something so fast with our lives, with the people around us. I kept talking to Firas: "Even though I'm not accomplishing anything yet, I feel a big relief. I'm here finally. Enough with the complaining. I'm not gonna keep crying all my life. I need to make things. I need to start all over and be the person that I've always been expected to be. Not just words, I don't want words. I'm not going to try our best, I'm going to *be* the best."

FIRAS: When Marwan got here, I was about to cry, that's for sure. I felt alive again. I could breathe. I felt like, "Okay, *now* I'm in the States. Now my mind is in the States, not somewhere else." It was like being home again, kinda. I found my new home on my own terms. I couldn't believe it. I was talking to Marwan and saying, "You don't know how long I've been waiting for you." He was laughing. "Why?"

I said, "Man, you don't know anything yet. You just got here. I will let you find out by yourself." He was laughing about it. I'm still figuring out the way of living, but day by day I'm learning more about how to live in the States. It was hard for Marwan to learn how to cross intersections—the traffic rules are totally different!

MARWAN: For us, there is always hope, or else you can't go on. Of course there is the hope we can go back to Baghdad, live there, see friends and family in Iraq, but we can't. I chose a band but at the cost of being an exile for the rest of my life. I'm still feeding on the hope that one day we'll be able to see our homeland again.

FAISAL RECEIVES JAMES HETFIELD'S GUITAR, PRUDENTIAL CENTER,
NEW JERSEY, FEBRUARY 1, 2009. PHOTO BY MONICA HAMPTON

EPILOGUE

On February 1, 2009, the band met Metallica backstage at a concert at the Prudential Center in Newark, New Jersey.

MARWAN: The people at *Vice* told us that we were going to meet Metallica. We just couldn't believe it. The titans of the metal world, and three days after I got here. We got the tickets and they said family and friends only, along with a band photo. We still couldn't believe it. We went to the concert and there were huge crowds cheering and we *still* couldn't believe it. Then we went backstage before the show and started seeing more amps and equipment and people carrying stuff, then it all sank in.

It kept getting more and more tense. We were all walking about in a big gang with the *Vice* guys, and then we came to the waiting room and the staff said, "Just wait down here."

Then someone from *Vice*, I guess it was Monica, said, "Oh shit! James Hetfield is here."

FAISAL: I couldn't handle it, because I've been listening to Metallica since I was in Baghdad and heard my first Metallica song when I was about eleven or twelve. It's been a long, long time. All these black market stores I used to buy their tapes at. I used to run when I heard some guy had their latest album for sale. All these moments were running through my head, they had all been so exciting in my own life and I wished all my friends were there. I'm so proud that I had this moment, even though it didn't last that long. James made it last. For us, shaking his hands and talking to him deeply, and he said, "You guys inspired us. You gave us another hope in this metal world." *James Hetfield* is telling us that we inspired him. Can you believe it? Marwan was doing all the talking because I couldn't speak. Firas was in complete chaos, shaking his head and talking a lot. Maybe Marwan had a little bit more courage to speak and spit it all out, but he was scared, too. I mean, we wouldn't have dreamed something like this could ever have happened.

I mean, seriously, each single word he said I could never forget. It kinda shocked me because in the moment when you're standing in front of one of the greatest bands on this planet, and he's actually been following *your* whole story—an Iraqi refugee group? I couldn't believe it.

After the show James came out with his flaming-sleeved robe and came toward us. We were all clapping like, "Right on!"

He just says, "Here, this is for you." And he gave me his Explorer, the finest guitar I think that anyone could have. He'd just been playing it onstage . . . you cannot imagine for how long I had been dreaming

THE BAND MEETS JAMES HETFIELD, PRUDENTIAL CENTER, NEW JERSEY,
FEBRUARY 1, 2009. PHOTO BY MONICA HAMPTON.

about this, not to touch it, God forbid, but to look at it in a glass box at one of those rock 'n' roll history museums, or something. That would be fair. But James Hetfield coming by himself and handing me his own guitar, which has been already played, with all his fingerprints on it, and he was putting it in my hands. I was like, "What the hell is happening? Guys? What does this man want from me? What the *fuck*?" He took a silver marker and he signed it: "Welcome to America! Love & respect, James Hetfield."

So it's James *and* his guitar *and* a signature with two of the most exciting and energetic words in the whole earth!

I prefer to see these words than to drink a whole case of Red Bull. I couldn't even say thank you, but I was speechless and choked.

THE BAND WITH JAMES HETFIELD'S GUITAR, PRUDENTIAL CENTER, NEW JERSEY, FEBRUARY 1, 2009. PHOTO BY SUROOSH ALVI.

THE BAND MEETS LARS ULRICH, PRUDENTIAL CENTER, NEW JERSEY,
FEBRUARY 1, 2009. PHOTOS BY MONICA HAMPTON.

TONY: A day after that, I called the guys. I saw the whole thing online so I already knew what had happened. Unfortunately, I had to be somewhere else so I could work on my family's refugee status. James giving them the guitar was amazing. I hope I'll be able to meet Metallica myself someday and I hope that now that we're surrounded by all these metal titans who appreciate our story and our dedication to what we love, we'll be able to start working on the band and be able to produce something.

MARWAN: Finally, now that our voice has been heard and our story told, I hope there's nothing to hold us back. Having those individuals, these legendary musicians on our side, having the people who support our cause, and who put their faith in us, I don't think we've done as much for them as they've done for us. By that I mean everyone. We just wanted to be a band and we've done this because we wanted to do it. And if going through all these unfortunate events and obstacles and zigzags is what we had to do, we succeeded. The final destination or not, this is our life and this is who we are. Through the war and the death and heartbreak and the hard times, we were always just a band.

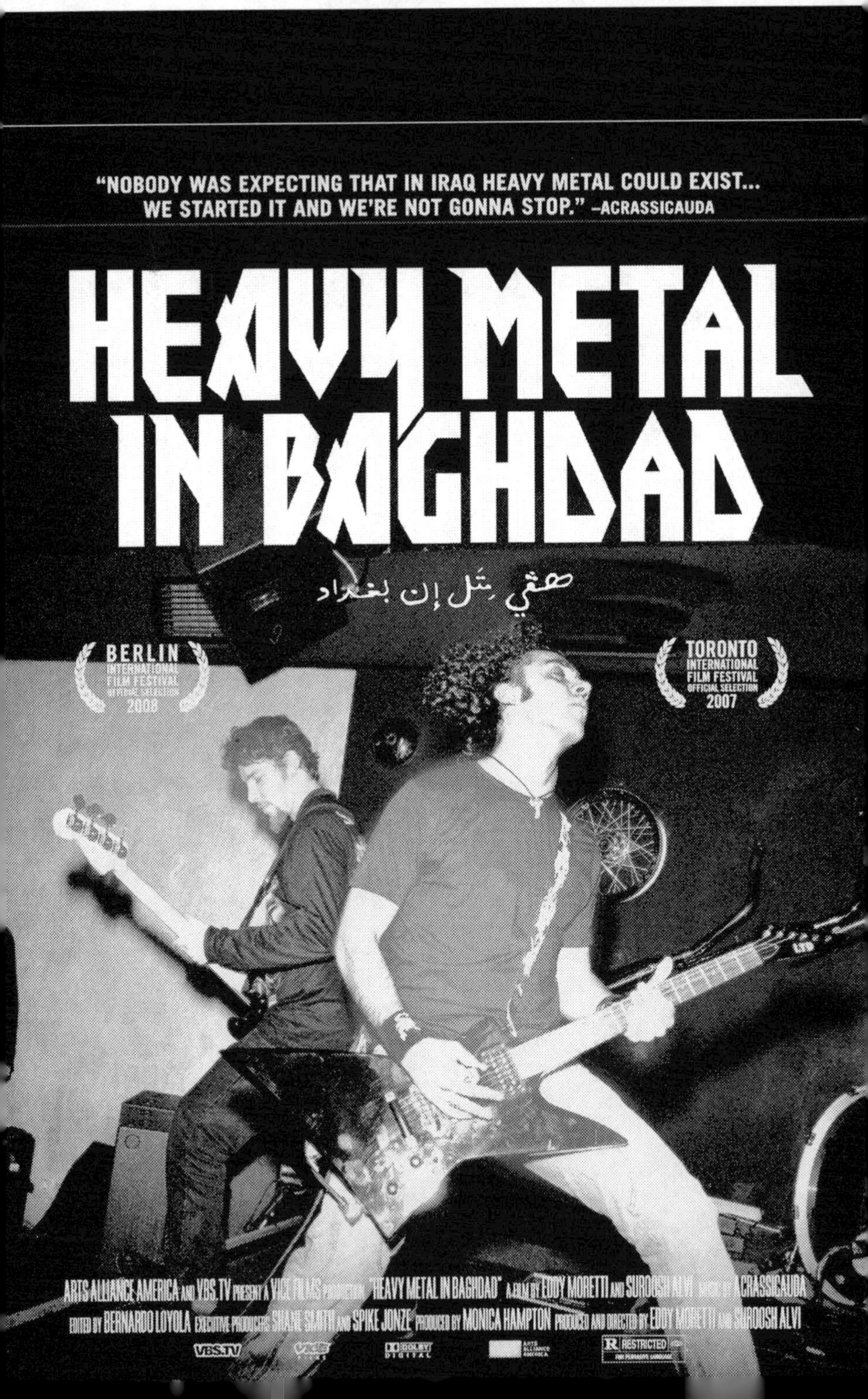

"Heavy Metal in Baghdad"
A Documentary Feature Film

Produced and Directed by
Suroosh Alvi

FINAL TRANSCRIPT

Produced by: Monica Hampton

[Start of movie]

<u>01:00:17:02</u>
ON SCREEN:
VBS.TV ANIMATION

<u>01:00:36:08</u>
TEXT ON SCREEN:
VICE FILMS

<u>01:00:48:28</u>
[Fade in: ext. Baghdad, Suroosh putting on bulletproof
vest]

[Music: Drums]

TEXT ON SCREEN:
AUGUST 2006

<u>01:00:54:16</u>
TEXT ON SCREEN:
VBS.TV PRESENTS
A VICE FILM PRODUCTION

Suroosh: Wanna put it on?

[Takes camera so Eddy can put on his vest]

<u>01:01:04:24</u>
TEXT ON SCREEN:
A FILM BY EDDY MORETTI

Suroosh: Nice and tight. Get that belly in there.

Eddy: Let's do this.

01:01:14:21
TEXT ON SCREEN:
AND SUROOSH ALVI

Suroosh: We're in Baghdad. We're here to interview the
only Iraqi heavy metal band, called Acrassicauda.

01:01:21:14
[Archival: Acrassicauda performing]

TEXT ON SCREEN:
ACRASSICAUDA

Suroosh (cont'd): We've been following them for three
years, and, um, we needed to check in on them, see if
they're still alive. This is risky, it's dangerous,
people would say it's really fucking stupid for us to be
doing this, but, um, you know . . . heavy metal rules.

01:01:38:06
[Music: Heavy metal music kicks in]

[Archival: Footage of Acrassicauda]

[Shot of Firas in Baghdad, next day]

Firas: Rock stars, yeah!

01:01:49:03
TEXT ON SCREEN:
FIRAS
BASS

Firas: I've been playing for almost, like, ten years
now, playing bass guitar. It's kind of a life for me. I

mean, I'm so crazy about it. I mean, I would rather play
than doing a lot of things in my life.

01:02:06:07
TEXT ON SCREEN:
TONY
LEAD GUITAR

01:02:08:23
Suroosh (off-camera): I wanna know how Tony got to be
so fucking good on the guitar.

[Archival: Band playing]

01:02:11:18
Tony (off-camera): (speaks in Arabic)

Tony (subtitled): Practicing.

Suroosh: How long has he been practicing for?

01:02:15:00
Tony: (speaks in Arabic)

Tony (subtitled): Eight years.

01:02:19:02
TEXT ON SCREEN:
MARWAN
DRUMS

01:02:22:08
Marwan: If you can teach every prisoner how to play
drum and smash drum, I believe that they will gonna
be turn out good citizens. I can't believe how much
this instrument helped me.

Marwan (subtitled): If you can teach every prisoner how
to play drums . . . smash drums . . . I believe that

they are gonna turn out to be good citizens. I can't
believe how much this instrument helped me.

01:02:36:01
TEXT ON SCREEN:
FAISAL
VOCALS/RHYTHM GUITAR

Suroosh (off-camera): How did you guys decide to
start a band, a metal band?

Faisal: If you really wanna know where's the
attraction, look around. We are living in a heavy
metal world.

01:02:48:03
[Archival: Shots of Baghdad being bombed at night,
intercut with footage of band playing—AP Archive
footage]

01:03:04:18
TEXT ON SCREEN:
HEAVY METAL IN BAGHDAD

01:03:18:03
[Music and footage fade out]

01:03:19:22
TEXT ON SCREEN:
NOVEMBER 2003

[New music starts]

Narration: Our relationship with this band started
in November of 2003, two and a half years before we
actually got to meet them.

01:03:28:03
[Archival: Saddam's statue, Saddam's statue toppling]

Narration (cont'd): Soon after the U.S. toppled Saddam
Hussein's regime, our friend Gideon Yago . . .

01:03:32:15
TEXT ON SCREEN:
GIDEON YAGO

Narration (cont'd): . . . got the opportunity to do
some reporting in Baghdad for MTV News. He brought us
an article called "No War for Heavy Metal" that we
published in our magazine, *Vice*.

01:03:36:20
[Archival: Shots of article in *Vice*]

Narration (cont'd): The article was about the challenges
that Acrassicauda faced being a heavy metal band in
Iraq, a country under the U.S.-led occupation and
on the verge of civil war. At the time there were
150,000 coalition troops in Iraq and they were failing
miserably. No electricity for the majority of Baghdad,
curfews at night, and the rise of the insurgency was the
backdrop for these poor musicians. They had to power
their amps with gas generators and carry guns to get to
their practice space.

[Archival: Shot montage]

01:03:42:29
LIVE SHOT OF ACRASSICAUDA

01:03:46:06
SOLDIER IN TANK

01:03:47:05
PROTESTORS IN THE STREET

01:03:49:29
TANKS DRIVING TOWARD CAMERA

01:03:53:16
SOLDIERS IN BACK OF TANK

01:03:59:15
INSURGENTS HOLDING GUNS

Narration (cont'd): While Gideon was in Baghdad, he met a twenty-year-old kid named Waleed, who at the time was the lead singer of Acrassicauda.

01:04:14:17
TEXT ON SCREEN:
WALEED

01:04:15:29
[Archival: Waleed singing onstage]

Narration (cont'd): He took Gideon to the band's practice space, a room in the basement of a commercial building in Karadah, a neighborhood in downtown Baghdad. Waleed, like the other guys in the band, practiced his English by watching American movies and listening to bootleg tapes of Slayer, Metallica, and Mayhem.

01:04:25:22
[Archival: Gideon with band in their basement practice space]

Gideon: So, guys, I wanted to ask, I mean the big question that I wanted to ask you guys is, I mean are you guys able to get gigs, you know, now that even with the situation being what it is? I mean can you even get people to come out to your shows, given that it's so . . .

Marwan: Yeah. It's like always. We have like three hundred, four hundred, sometimes five hundred.

Gideon: So have you guys had a concert since the war?

Waleed: Since the war? We did a show . . . well,
actually, one, two, three shows we did.

Gideon: Are you guys afraid of anything right now?

Gideon (subtitled): Are you guys afraid of anything
right now?

Marwan: Right now? For me, I don't give a fuck. I don't
know about these guys.

Marwan (subtitled): For me, I don't give a fuck. I don't
know about you guys.

Faisal: I'm afraid of what's gonna happen on the concert
[laughs], of the kind of audience that's gonna be.

Faisal (subtitled): I'm afraid of what's gonna happen at
the concert, of the kind of audience that's gonna be.

Marwan: Ah, fuck that shit.

Marwan (subtitled): Fuck that shit.

Marwan: If I was walking down the street and someone
throw a bunch of grenades, some crazy motherfucker,
and like he just like bomb me, tear me from pieces,
I'd be afraid from that, 'cause like I didn't do
anything in my life, I'm still young. You know?

Marwan (subtitled): I was afraid, like, if I was
walking down the street and someone threw a bunch
of grenades. Some crazy motherfucker. And like . . .
he just like . . . bomb me, tear me to pieces.
I would be afraid from that. 'Cause like I didn't do
anything in my life. I'm still young. You know?

Gideon: Would you guys ever think of writing a song
now that's like an anti-Saddam song, or . . . ?

209

Marwan: We are not a politic band. We are not like
System of a Down or something. We got to like stay
away from the politic, 'cause like for me, if I was
like watching some like series or something, a movie,
and like some guy shown up and tried like say news or
something—I'll turn on the channel. 'Cause like for me,
I don't give a fuck about the news.

Marwan (subtitled): We are not a politic band. We're
not like System of a Down or something. We gotta like
stay away from the politics. 'Cause like for me, if I
was like watching some like series or something, or a
movie and some guy shown up and tried like say news or
something—I'll turn off the channel. 'Cause like for
me, I don't give a fuck about the news.

Gideon: You guys just want to rock.

Marwan: Yeah.

[Music: Acrassicauda practicing]

Waleed (singing): Yeah, yeah, motherfucker, you're
gonna die.

01:06:47:03
[Fade out]

01:06:51:06
Narration: A few months after that interview, Waleed left
the band. Through some friends outside the country, he
managed to get a student visa and fled Iraq for art school
in Canada. Waleed and the others have not spoken since.

01:07:03:01
[Music: Rock]

01:07:04:16
TEXT ON SCREEN:
JULY 2005

01:07:08:05
TEXT ON SCREEN:
TWO YEARS LATER

01:07:15:01
[Int. apartment; Faisal picks up cellphone from table]

Faisal: Hey, what's up, dude?

Narration: We stayed in touch with Acrassicauda, and
in the summer of 2005, we organized a concert with them
in central Baghdad at the Al-Fanar Hotel.

[Ext. shots of Baghdad from car; front of hotel]

01:07:22:16
TEXT ON SCREEN:
AL-FANAR HOTEL

Narration (cont'd): The plan was for Eddy and I to fly
in from Beirut, but two bombs went off, the airport got
shut down, and we were stuck in Lebanon.

[Footage of Lebanon from plane, then on the ground]

01:07:27:06
TEXT ON SCREEN:
BEIRUT, LEBANON

Narration (cont'd): At that point, it was too late to
cancel the show, so we got in touch with our friend
Johan Spanner, a Danish photojournalist who'd been
living in Baghdad for a year and a half.

01:07:38:11
TEXT ON SCREEN:
JOHAN SPANNER

Narration: He became our man on the ground, and when
the show finally went off, we were sitting in Beirut, five

hundred miles away. Organizing the show was a logistical
nightmare. Because of the Al-Fanar's proximity to
the green zone, the level of security was incredibly
high. The hotel was basically encapsulated by blast
walls and barbed wire, and tanks were stationed right
outside the door. Every piece of the band's equipment
had to be examined to make sure that no bombs were
being smuggled in, and the show had to be over by seven
o'clock, so the fans could get home before the curfew
went into effect.

01:08:22:14
[Int. hotel lobby, sitting with band]

Johan (off-camera): So tell me about the band name.

Firas: The band name is actually a scientific term, it's
in a Latin language, uh, Acrassicauda, which is mean
"the black scorpion," which is the most, you know, as
you know, the most dangerous scorpion, you can find it
in a desert, like an Iraqi desert or Kuwaiti desert.

01:08:25:01
TEXT ON SCREEN:
FIRAS BASS
TONY LEAD GUITAR

[Shots of band setting up to play at hotel]

Marwan: I never felt like I was gonna like play with my
band again. I mean like we're not even like had a chance
to practice together, since like we got the threat, a
threat.

01:08:46:17
TEXT ON SCREEN:
MARWAN DRUMS

Johan (off-camera): What kind of threat was that?

[Music]

Marwan: We had a threat like saying we're like
Americanized, and like we're playing music for Satan and
stuff, blah blah blah. "We're gonna get you one by one,"
"You're gonna fall down," and shit.

[Cut back to sitting in hotel lobby]

01:09:04:26
Marwan: We were raised up like with Metallica songs and
the other stuff.

Marwan (subtitled): We were raised up with Metallica
songs and the other stuff . . .

Faisal: We were raised up on music. It's time we created
the band, we just wanted to be one of our band heroes, I
mean, like or the best guitar players, the best bands in
the world, best vocalist, and we always dreamed up that we
gonna have a tour with them or some stuff like that, you
know. Any young man could have a dreams for his future.

01:09:07:28
TEXT ON SCREEN:
FAISAL VOCALS
AHMED GUEST RHYTHM GUITAR

Marwan: Let's say like we're twenty-two, twenty-three,
twenty-five, so this is like they say like "spring of
your age," whatever . . .

Firas: Our parents . . .

Marwan: Like this is the time you do your hobbies,
go . . . I mean like I was gonna say go get drunk, go to
the nightclubs, just like let's say like a decent life
for twenty-five-years-old-age guy, and like I ain't got

213

nothing. We can't do a lot when people outside. Just like you got a civil war outside, just like accept like that you're taking care of your family and you're real careful of your family.

01:09:57:08
Marwan (subtitled): We can't do a lot when people outside just like . . . you got a civil war outside.

[Footage of tanks, armed personnel roaming Baghdad streets]

Firas: Every time I go out, you know, I start thinking about, okay, what if I got killed now, and what about my wife, what about if I gonna have a baby soon or something like that, and what's gonna happen to my kid? I don't want my kid to grow up in this, I mean, situation, circumstances here. I'm trying my best to get out of this country, to go somewhere where I can find peace for me and my family, I mean, that's my personal thought.

Marwan: Personal, for me, I got shot before like two weeks, my car . . .

Firas (off-camera): He got his car shot at.

Marwan: My mom, she's a primary school teacher, and like I was like just getting my mom from the school back to the house. And like, "Boom!" The guy shot me.

Faisal: We face up this kind of situation all the time.

Marwan: Every single day, every single day. You got the troops and you got the terrorist outside, and we are stuck in the middle.

01:11:00:15
Marwan (subtitled): You got the troops and you got the terrorists outside, and we are stuck in the middle.

214

Marwan: I'm a civilian, I've done nothing in my life,
I didn't steal, I didn't kill, I didn't do nothing.
That's the democracy that we got now. So, I'm like,
"Fuck this democracy."

01:11:22:25
Johan: So you guys played concerts, uh, during the, the
former regime, as well, right?

Johan (subtitled): So, but you guys played concerts
during the former regime as well, right?

Firas: Yes, yeah, yeah.

Firas (subtitled): Yes, yeah.

Johan: So how did, how did that work out?

Johan (subtitled): So how did that work out?

01:11:29:13
Firas: Um, we went to the Culture and Media
Ministry. So they said, Okay, what are you gonna play?
We said, Hey, we gonna play rock, whatever. They
said, Okay, what you got for, you know, Saddam or
the regime? And, if we gonna play without having a
song for Saddam, the security, whatever, would
capture you and put you in a jail for no reason,
because they don't really understand what you're
doing. So we said, Okay, I mean, yeah, we'll play
a song for Saddam.

Firas (subtitled): We went to the Culture and Media
Ministry.

So, they said, Okay, what are you gonna play?
We said we are gonna play rock, whatever.

They said, Okay, what you got for, you know, Saddam, or
the regime?

215

And if we are gonna play without having a song for
Saddam, the security, whatever, would capture you,
and put you in a jail for no reason. Because they don't
really understand what you are doing.

So we said, Okay, I mean, yeah. We'll play a song for
Saddam.

Faisal: Well, the tune wasn't shit but the lyrics . . .
I mean . . .

Faisal (subtitled): Well, the tune wasn't shit, but the
lyrics . . . I mean . . .

01:12:02:08
[Archival: Band performing]

01:12:04:24
TEXT ON SCREEN:
[AL-ORFALY] HALL, 2002
STILL UNDER SADDAM'S POWER

"THE YOUTH OF IRAQ"

Waleed (singing): *Livin' in the dark, shining like a spark,
living with the pride, so we decide, to fight the evil
forces, yeah. We won't accept it, we're never gonna lose,
following our leader, Saddam Hussein, we will make them
fall, make them go insane, following our leader, Saddam
Hussein, we'll make them fall, we will drive them insane.*

01:12:09:05
Waleed (subtitled):

Living in the dark,
shining like a spark.

Living with pride,
so we decide
to fight the evil forces. Yeah.

216

We won't accept it,
we're never gonna lose.

Following our leader, Saddam Hussein,

We'll make them fall,
we will drive them insane.

Following our leader, Saddam Hussein,

We'll make them fall,
we will drive them insane.

01:12:25:06
Firas (off-camera): You know, just a bunch of fucking
lies and shit. But you gotta do it anyway, so, you know.
Like an Arabic saying we got, you know, "To stay away
from the devil, sing for it."

Firas (subtitled): You know, just a bunch of fucking
lies and shit. But you gotta do it anyway, so . . .
you know. Like an Arabic saying we got: "To stay away
from the devil, sing for him."

[Back to int. sitting on couches]

Firas: Nobody was allowed to do headbangs and stuff,
because they were concerned as a, you know, whatever,
religious practice, just like Jews, with I mean Jewish
prayer, you know what I'm saying, when the Jewish
they pray, they shake their heads and stuff. So they
think that's, the headbanging is related to this, and
that's, the headbanging itself could take you to jail
forever.

Johan: Really?

Firas: Yeah, I mean, so a lot of people, they were,
I mean, so scared to do it. I hope I live, you know,
somewhere else, not in Iraq, so I can get long hair,

long beard, Zakk Wylde-style thing, you know what I'm saying?

01:13:02:02
Firas (subtitled): I hope I live, you know, somewhere else, not in Iraq, so I can get long hair, long beard, Zakk Wylde-style thing.

01:13:08:18
[Archival: Photograph of Zakk Wylde]

TEXT ON SCREEN:
ZAKK WYLDE GUITAR HERO

Firas: Here, I mean, you can't really, with this goatee, I get in, you know, a lot of troubles.

Johan: Do you think a lot of chicks are gonna show up?

01:13:15:12
Johan: Do you think any chicks are gonna show up?

Firas: Could be.

Marwan: Yeah.

Firas: Hey, what about your girlfriend?

Marwan: No fucking way, man.

Firas: What? Come on!

Marwan: As I said, man, we got sixty horny motherfuckers were gonna show up down there. 'Cause we got tradition, culture. So like they are not gonna show up.

[Shots of people gathered outside, intercut with scenes from int.]

Johan: So right now we are facing some problems at the gate and fucking security that we've double-checked with like fucking five times over won't let our folks in, so . . .

Off-screen: Why won't they let them in?

Johan: Probably because they look like they do. Like with Iron Maiden T-shirts and so on.

01:13:31:13
[Cut back to outside of hotel, followed by walking to security gate and shots of security gate and walk back.]

Firas: No filming.

01:13:53:28
Off-screen: It's off, it's off. You guys don't have to worry about it. Okay. Bye-bye.

Off-screen (subtitled): It's off, don't worry about it.

Off-screen: We have to talk to coalition forces again.

Off-screen: I know we talked to them yesterday, but we have to do it again.

01:14:12:24
Soldier (into walkie-talkie): Roger, I have a man here. They are having, uh . . . They are playing tonight. [now to them] As long as they have their picture ID and it's legal . . . not a problem.

Soldier (subtitled): Roger. I have a man here. They are having, uh . . . They are playing tonight. As long as they have their picture ID and it's legal, not a problem.

Firas: Okay, that's cool for us. Hey, thank you, guys. Appreciate it . . . I know you talked to them yesterday, but these guys keep forgetting stuff, you know? I mean, they don't really.

01:14:39:22
[Shots of band, int. hotel, setting up for concert]

Marwan: Basically everything is set up. We're done for now. We're like, I would say like one hundred percent ready for the concert.

Marwan (subtitled): Basically everything is set up. We're done for now. We are like, I would say like one hundred percent ready for the concert.

Faisal: Now, this—

01:14:56:22
Band collectively (subtitled): Power failure.

Faisal (subtitled): Great.

[Int. shots away from equipment]

Faisal: We gonna have the conference on a generator. An old hotel generator. This is not good. This is not good, completely not good.

Faisal (subtitled): We are gonna have the concert on a generator. An old hotel generator.

01:15:10:25
[Johan standing with band]

Johan: So, uh, when did you play your last concert?

Marwan: A year from now, man.

Marwan (subtitled): A year from now, man [a year ago].

Firas: I mean, people want, people want what we can't . . .

Johan: Right.

Firas: But I mean, we can't find—

Marwan: People like, Dude! Is it safe? I was like, Yeah!
No one gonna blow us up? I was like, I'm hoping man.

Johan: The guys you invited, or—

Marwan: Yeah. I'm like, I'm hoping.

Johan: If we go, we go together.

Marwan: Yeah.

Firas: Metalheads forever.

01:15:38:20
[Cut to black; sound of bomb exploding]

[Cut back to hotel interior]

Off-screen: Did you guys hear something a minute ago?

Tony: What was that?

Tony (subtitled): What was that?

Off-screen: If I'm gonna hear another one—

01:15:54:14
Marwan: Impact. It was an impact.

Marwan (subtitled): Impact. It was an impact.

01:15:56:24
Off-screen: Was that a car bomb or a mortar?

Off-screen (subtitled): Was that a car bomb or
a mortar?

Marwan: No, mortar round.

Marwan (subtitled): No, a mortar round.

Off-screen: Mortar round?

Marwan: Yeah.

01:16:04:00
Firas: Everybody start calling me. Seeing if we still
'live or not.

Firas (subtitled): Everybody start calling me to see
if we are still alive or not.

Off-screen: Are they?

Firas: Yeah. [laughing]

01:16:13:11
[Band on couch]

Firas: I mean, we got used to it because we seen it
every day, on TV, in the streets everywhere, we got used
to seeing dead people everywhere. So it's just kind of
nothing now, for us, I mean, explosions as, as you know,
we've been hearing something happen, some explosion
happening. It's nothing. We keep playing.

01:16:28:00
[Cut back to concert space]

Marwan: But like we still, we still doing that concert.
We still . . .

01:16:32:11
[Band gathers in circle, joins hands in center]

Band (in Arabic): Long live Acrassicauda. Long live.

Band (subtitled): Long live Acrassicauda. Long live.

Bandmate: Let's go! Let's go! Let's go!

01:16:36:17
[Shots of audience outside and arriving into hotel.
Crowd shots int. hotel]

[Music: Band plays "Poison Tree"]

01:16:42:08
[Concert at hotel]

01:16:58:04
[Intercuts concert footage with that of interview with
band on couch]

Marwan: It just feel like you been like caged, like
there's chains, all around you. So like we wanna
for two hours or for three hours, practice time or
like the live performance, we wanna free ourselves
from that chain. Just like get that rage out.
Like sometimes, if I didn't play drums as hard as
I can, as fast as I can, I gonna kill someone.
I gonna—each one of us will turn to be a killing
machine.

01:17:20:00
[Back to concert at hotel]

[Music: Band playing]

01:17:28:00
[Power cuts out]

Off-screen: What's going on?

01:17:34:14
Audience Member 1: The electricity is gone off. There
is no fucking elec—electricity.

Audience Member 1 (subtitled): The electricity is gone
off. There is no fucking electricity.

01:17:40:14
Audience Member 2: We are of the heavy metal of music.
We are in the Iraq. Nobody here can grow, er, the long
hair. You know? Because, er, they will think we are, er,
the bad guys. So, we need real freedom.

Audience Member 2 (subtitled): We are of the heavy metal
of music.

We are in the Iraq.

Nobody here can grow the long hair, you know?

Because they will think we are the bad guys.

So, we need real freedom.

01:17:57:00
Audience Member 3: If we cannot find some fun here, so
where? Somebody answer me. You? You cannot.

Audience Member 3 (subtitled): If we cannot find some fun
here, so where? Somebody answer me. You? You cannot.

Off-screen: I can't.

Audience Member 3: Oh, we are fine now!

Audience Member 3 (subtitled): Oh, we are fine now.

01:18:06:23
Faisal: Okay, the next song is gone be one of our fucking songs, saddest songs. Okay, is called, fuckin' "Massacre"!
Faisal (subtitled): Okay. The next song is gonna be one of our fucking songs . . . saddest songs. Okay. This is called "Massacre."

[Music: band plays "Massacre"]

Faisal: Stop with the fucking lights and let's do it!

Faisal: *It's gone, It's our nation. It's our generation. Change of devolution. Enjoy your devolution. Massacre of a generation and the devil is still waiting. They want war for the rest of the future. They say you don't need it much longer. They want the war and you want the peace. But you know you gotta kill the beast. They stole my lands. They stole my home. They stole my flesh. They stole my bones. One step for victory. One step for death.*

Faisal (subtitled):

It's gone.

It's our nation.

It's our generation.

Change of devolution.

Enjoy your devolution.

Massacre of a generation

And the devil is still waiting.

They want war for the rest of the future.

They say you don't need it much longer.

They want the war and you want the peace.

But you know you gotta kill the beast.

They stole my lands.
They stole my home.
They stole my flesh.
They stole my bones.

One step for victory.

One step for death.

<u>01:19:46:10</u>
[Shot of Johan, ext. shots nighttime, footage from concert]

Narration: Despite all the challenges and difficulties of setting this concert up, and the war that was going on everywhere outside of the confines of this hotel, the show went off. The fans that came had a great time and they had a brief reprieve from the violence that was surrounding their lives, and after that show Acrassicauda would never play in Baghdad again.

<u>01:20:08:00</u>
[Music fades back in, screen fades out]

TEXT ON SCREEN:
AUGUST 2006
ONE YEAR LATER

<u>01:20:19:00</u>
[Ext. shot of airplane landing]

[Music: Instrumental]

TEXT ON SCREEN:
FRANKFURT INTERNATIONAL AIRPORT
GERMANY

01:20:22:00
Narration: Our obsession with the band continued to
grow. Finally, after a year of deliberation.

[Int. Frankfurt Airport, shots of Eddy Moretti and
Suroosh Alvi in airport]

Narration: In August of 2006, when Iraq was basically
in full-blown civil war, Eddy and I decided to go to
Baghdad to track these guys down and see if they were
still alive.

[Archival: Still of band]

Eddy: We bought a six hundred-and-ten-dollar Euro
ticket one way to Erbil in Kurdistan. This plane brings
us there tomorrow morning. It's really difficult to
get visas. They wouldn't even let me in the door of
the embassy. But this is what we're doing.

01:20:51:16
[World map]

TEXT ON SCREEN:

    Germany
    Frankfurt

    Erbil   Iraqi Kurdistan Region
    Baghdad
    Iraq

Eddy (cont'd): We flew here to Frankfurt to get the
only flight into Erbil from Europe and apparently
you can buy your visa on the ground in Erbil in the

227

airport. It's just a massive loophole in Iraq and it's called Kurdistan.

Suroosh: Smuggling ourselves into Iraq through the loophole and with no way to get to Baghdad.

[Shot of people in airport, back to Suroosh]

Suroosh: We'll fly, but we don't know when.
Suroosh [reading *Time* article]: "To avoid being shot down by Iraqi insurgents, the pilot must stay at nine thousand meters until the plane is directly over Baghdad Airport, then bank into a spiraling dive straightening up just meters from the runway. If you are looking out the window it can feel as if the plane is in a free fall from which it possibly can't pull out. The only thing worse than the view from the window is being seated next to someone who hasn't taken the flight before. During one especially difficult landing in 2004, a retired American cop wouldn't stop screaming, 'Oh God, oh God.' I finally had to slap him in the face on instructions from the flight attendant."

01:21:54:00
[Shot of *Time* magazine cover]

Eddy: It's today's pa—

Suroosh: Today's . . .

Both: Today's . . .

Suroosh: *Time* magazine. Uh, with "A Baghdad Diary." And it's probably not the best thing to be looking at before flying to Iraq. I feel sick to my stomach. I was feeling calm about this trip and now I'm shitting bricks. Thanks. I'm freaking out.

01:22:01:00
[Zoom to close-up shot of *Time* magazine cover]

01:22:13:14
[Music fades in: Drums]

01:22:15:24
[Suroosh on plane, shots from plane, shots of Erbil
airport, people on tarmac]

**Narration: We land in Erbil and we walk to the
Customs and Immigration people . . .**

01:22:25:00
TEXT ON SCREEN:
ERBIL INTERNATIONAL AIRPORT
IRAQI KURDISTAN

**Narration (cont'd): . . . and they just stamped our
passport and they just let us in. Eddy was filming as we
walked off the plane. We hired a taxi and about a mile
later . . .**

[Shots from car, shots of soldiers, shot of man with
camera]

**Narration (cont'd): . . . we get pulled over by a bunch
of guys with guns. That's how we entered Iraq, being
questioned and going through the camera and being
forced to erase everything that we've shot this far.**

01:22:45:00
[Screen goes black]

Off-screen: How many minutes did you recorded?

Eddy (off-camera): About two minutes. Just from here to
there.

Off-screen: Okay.

01:22:51:00
[Int. car, day, shots of scenery outside]

Narration: There were two ways to get to Baghdad from Erbil: driving or flying. And due to the rise of the insurgency and the roadside bombs, we decided to fly after spending a night in Erbil. The corkscrew landing was actually not such a big deal. The Americans have expanded the perimeter around the airport and instead of doing a nosedive, the pilots do these big, wide circles as they land.

01:23:12:15
[Shot of Baghdad International Airport]

TEXT ON SCREEN:
BAGHDAD INTERNATIONAL AIRPORT

01:23:15:00
[Suroosh stands outside airport]

Suroosh: As soon as we arrived at the airport, the first question they asked us was: "Have you guys ever used guns?" And then they gave us these flak jackets and they said, "Be prepared to be shot at, uh, you'll probably have snipers shooting at you." And they said, "Your car is full of guns." This is basically a gangster's paradise. There are people getting kidnapped every day. Um, there's upward of three hundred people getting killed every day.

[Suroosh gets into car]

Suroosh (cont'd): All right. You're not allowed to wear seatbelts here because it's an obvious giveaway that you're a foreigner.

01:23:42:27
[Shots of Baghdad from int. car]

Suroosh (cont'd): So we're driving down the highway of death right now. It's a seven-mile stretch from, directly from the airport to the green zone and it's

the most dangerous seven miles of road in the world.
Snipers, uh, roadside bombs, badness, et cetera. And
he's doing this weird zigzagging.

Eddy (off-camera): It's really, really, really
off-putting.

Narration: We followed a lead through Al-Jazeera and
Reuters. We found an Iraqi security company. And for
$1,500 a day, we'll get a bulletproof SUV, another
car without armor, two drivers, two shooters, and one
translator. That's a steal.

01:24:37:00
[Ext. in front of cars, putting on vests]

Ahmed (off-camera): We have a custom here, an, eh, every
morning when we woke up from the bed, we said, "Good
morning, Baghdad." It mean that there is a new bomb in
Baghdad.

Ahmed (subtitled): We have a custom here, every
morning when we wake up from the bed, we say, "Good
morning, Baghdad." It means that there is a new bomb
in Baghdad.

[Music: Middle Eastern]

01:24:49:26
TEXT ON SCREEN:
AHMED

[Shots of Ahmed, int. of car, shots of security guard
standing by cars, Ahmed sitting inside]

Narration: This is Ahmed. He was our fixer. He was our
translator. He was the guy that we would call and
arrange all of our Baghdad excursions and he begged us
not to show you his face because we'll put his life at
risk if we do that.

01:25:09:12
[Shots of helicopter and Baghdad from int. of car]

01:25:12:00
Suroosh: That's the Al-Fanar hotel, where we had our
Vice concert in Baghdad last summer. Then they bombed
it. They threw grenades into it . . .

Suroosh (subtitled): That's the Al-Fanar hotel, where we
had the *Vice* concert in Baghdad last summer. Then they
bombed it. They threw grenades into it . . .

Ahmed (off-camera): Be sure that no one can see you.

Ahmed (subtitled): Be sure that no one can see you.

01:25:24:03
[Shots of mosques from int. of car]

[Music fades out]

01:25:34:23
[Int. of car]

Suroosh: Hello, Firas? As-Salamu Alaykum.

Suroosh (subtitled): As-Salamu Alaykum.

Suroosh: So it's, uh, 9:25 and we're in the
neighborhood. We'll be there soon. Are you there? He
hung up on me. One of the most dangerous things is
speaking English on the street. So he was whispering
into the phone. All he said was, "Okay . . . okay."

01:26:13:29
TEXT ON SCREEN:
AL-HAMRA HOTEL COMPOUND

Suroosh: The entrance to this hotel is really sketchy.

232

Ahmed (off-camera): [speaks in Arabic]

Eddy (off-camera): His name is Firas.

Suroosh: We're meeting someone named Firas, who's in there waiting.

Soldier: [speaks in Arabic]

01:26:26:00
[Ext. walking through hotel compound]

Narration: Although we'd been in touch with the band for two and a half years, this was the first time we'd met any of them face-to-face, and we needed to gain his trust, so we had to meet Firas on his terms, at a place where he felt safe.

01:26:40:00
[Int. hotel, interview with Firas]

Firas: What's up, dudes?

[Laughter]

Firas (cont'd): Yeah, so.

Eddy: So, so, and this is the lobby of the hotel here?

Firas: Uh, this is the cafeteria, the lobby is out there. And it's the Hamra hotel. I don't know if you guys are familiar with it but most of the reporters comes here.

01:26:59:21
[Archival: Wreckage outside hotel after car bombing]

Firas (cont'd): This got a blowed up last year by a car bomb.

[Archival: Soldiers outside, wreckage of building]

Firas (cont'd): I was here. That was a big mess,
I mean . . .

[Archival: Wide shot of building rubble after bomb and
crowds of civilians]

Firas (cont'd): Took a whole like fucking three, four
houses totally destroyed, I mean . . . you know?

Firas (subtitled): It's the Hamra Hotel. I don't
know if you guys are familiar with it . . . but
most of the reporters come here. This got blown
up by a car bomb. I was here. It was a big mess,
I mean . . . took a whole fucking, like . . .
three or four houses. Totally destroyed, I mean . . .
you know?

Suroosh: Are you working right now?

Firas: Yeah. I got a little computer store downtown in
the city.

Suroosh: Are there any other metal bands right now?

Firas: No. There's, there's projects, you know, for
metal bands and, but nobody, nobody could make it.

Suroosh: When we, when we first wrote about you, we said
that you were the only . . . only metal band in Iraq.

Firas: We still the only. There was a projects but no
bands formed yet. It just—what I mean by, what I meant
by projects, you know, a couple guys here—

Suroosh: Jamming here.

234

Firas: Jamming, couple guys there jamming. But nobody have made it yet to get up on the stage and—

Suroosh: But did you think that when Saddam was in power, that if he was taken away, that everyone would just start killing everyone else?

Firas: No. I thought that everything would be better.

Suroosh: Right.

Firas: Actually, in the beginning, I mean, in the beginning, everything was getting better, but later on, I mean, I don't know what happened. Like the, let us say the first year, you know, it's kind of like there's a couple incidents here and there but nothing much against people. Now's everything going against people, you know. Now what the people say about us, they, you know, they took one thief, you know they took Ali Baba, and they left the forty thief. Which is what we have now. Which is, I don't know who the hell they are, but anyway.

Suroosh: Various militias.

Firas: Ehh, whatever, dude, I mean you got, you got like fuckin', I don't know like a thousand of fucking different type of fucking militia and forces and army and police and I don't know what the hell it is. And you know, people come from Syria, Iraq, Turkey, uh, Kuwait, Saudi Arabia, all over the fucking place, they come here.

01:28:40:00
Suroosh: To fight jihad.

Suroosh (subtitled): To fight jihad.

Firas: Dude, there is nothing about jihad, okay. It's all fucking politic bullshit. I mean, dude, I'm Muslim and I'm telling you. There is nothing about jihad think against Christian or crusade or against Jewish or nothing like that. I mean, all the people who's dying here in Iraq are just Muslims, dude.

Suroosh: Yeah.

Firas: Dude, that's—

Suroosh: American media is saying that it's sectarian violence, a lot of the insurgents.

Firas: Dude, that's what you hear on TV, it's nothing related to the facts. I mean, dude, I'm a Sunni, my wife is Shia. This is a totally fake truth, or whatever, media, fucking propaganda shit. I feel kind of like the government is forcing . . . or not the government, but the people, like the politicians, is kind of forcing this racist thing between Shia and Sunni. Shia don't hate Sunni or Sunnis don't hate Shia. That's, uh . . .

Suroosh: Have you thought about going to Jordan? With your family?

Firas: Yeah, I thought about it but, dude, in Jordan they treat you like shit.

Suroosh: Really?

Firas: Yeah, if you're Iraqi, dude, a couple months ago I was thinking about going to Syria but now I have a baby. It's just like, you know, I have to wait a little while, you know. Let the baby grow a little bit.

Suroosh: Yeah.

Eddy (off-camera): So you've never left Baghdad?

Firas: Who, me? Yeah, I told you farthest I've been from Baghdad is Baghdad itself.

Suroosh: Could you grow your hair long now that Saddam is out?

Firas: Ah, no, I get trouble for this goatee, dude. That's why I'm trying to grow it as a beard.

Suroosh: Like a proper Islamic beard.

Firas: Yeah, kind of, you know, but I mean, it's not, uh, I got nothing against religion, you know, I'm a Muslim, but I'm not that straight, dude, I mean, just, I'm a regular person. Dude, I mean I'm at a big risk right now wearing this T-shirt because it's an American band and it's like a . . . that could get you killed in Baghdad. We got an Arabic saying that people always enemy for what they don't know. So basically they fighting this because they don't know what the hell it is.

Suroosh: What does your wife say?

Firas: About what?

Suroosh: About the fact that you're taking a risk, wearing the shirt, I mean, that you have facial hair.

Firas: Uh, I mean, she . . . she's totally, she totally understands it.

Suroosh: Cool.

Firas: Yeah, she's cool with it. She says, I mean we all, you know, live under all these circumstances. Just like being a soldier living in a war. You could die at any second. So no matter what, you're wearing your helmet or not, you're going to get shot, I mean. So it's the same thing. I mean, I wear this, I wear that, I wear whatever, I go there, here. I mean I believe in my destiny. If it's my time, it's my time, it's my turn, so that's it.

Suroosh: But you're ready to die?

Firas: Yeah, I'm ready to die. You know, just like.
It's just you know, when you reach this level of being
hopeless you know you just, you go cool with it. You
live your life. You live every moment you've got. And
then you don't think about when you're gonna die, you
just . . . I'm living today.

01:31:29:11
[Firas holding Iron Maiden CD in front of him]

Firas: This is what life looks like here. [laughing]
Death on the Road, dude.

01:31:38:10
[Shot of getting back into car with gun. Shots of
Baghdad from car, int. car at night, balcony overlooking
Baghdad at night]

[Hard rock music fades in]

Narration: My experience in Baghdad is what I imagined
prison to be like. I have never experienced a level
of fear and paranoia so high anywhere. Where no one
trusts anybody, everyone is watching their back, you
know, Baghdad is on lockdown. They have a curfew at
nine o'clock every night, you have to be indoors. So
we'd drive around during the day, check out carnage and
destruction, and then come back to our hotel. We'd sit
on our balcony, we'd smoke cigarettes and we'd look out
into the darkness and we'd see flames and the occasional
bomb going off and Apache helicopters flying right by our
hotel. It was an incredibly surreal experience.

01:32:16:11
[View from balcony; bomb explodes in distance]

Eddy (off-camera): Whoa.

Narration: The nights were hot. It was like somebody was holding a fucking hairdryer to your face at all times.

[Music fades]

<u>01:32:31:21</u>
[Int. hotel]

Eddy (off-camera): Just be honest, can we go anywhere in this city?

Firas: No. On your own, no. I don't guarantee it.

Suroosh: Did we make a mistake by coming here?

Firas: [laughing] Yeah, I don't know. It's, it's, it's, you know, it's kind of, yes, I mean, it's kind of hard for you guys. I mean, I don't really know what to say, but . . .

I mean, I . . . I . . . I . . . I understand your job and I respect you because you sacrifice yourself just to do something, or I mean, just to let the people in the world know what the hell is going on in this country. But, at the same time, it's just a crazy mission, dude.

<u>01:33:05:15</u>
[Shots of Baghdad from int. of car]

[Music: instrumental]

Suroosh: We haven't seen any journalists around. We've seen two camera crews, but they've been filming inside of our hotel. So they send out Iraqi camera crews to film an incident and then the Western journalists just talk over it and say, "Twelve people were killed when this bomb went off in a market." It's really, virtually impossible to do any kind of real reporting in the streets because you can't, you can't talk—

Eddy (off-camera): You can't meet Iraqis.

Suroosh: You can't, you can't meet Iraqis. They're afraid of you. They run from you when they see you and you're an instant target.

Narration: After four days of being inside of armored cars and secured compounds, we convinced our security to take us to an open, unguarded area on the edge of the Tigris River.

01:34:13:06
[Ext. standing along river]

Suroosh: So if you, if you look right there, that's our hotel in the background, and every night after curfew, we sit out and we look over the city and for the last two nights, right where we're standing, there's been a firefight. Cars driving, people shooting at each other, and, um, and today we, uh, we drove here, and it's the first time that we're standing out in the street, uh, filming, and they say it's safe now, uh, but I, you know, I beg to differ because, uh, there's been so much activity here.

Soldier: (speaks in Arabic)

Suroosh: Most of these guys, some of them are army guys, but a lot of them are engineers, and teachers, and they get trained, and now they're working as, as bodyguards. It's the only way to make money and they lie about it, so none of their friends know they do this, they leave in the morning and say, "I'm off to work in the shop today," and they go and they pick up their AK, and they drive around, and they risk losing their lives every single day.

01:35:17:00
[Ext. by the river]

Ahmed: It is not safe, we can't bring you here. So
we are not allowed to stay here. But the snipers, we
don't know where they be.

Ahmed (subtitled): It is not safe, we can't bring
you here. So we are not allowed to stay here. The
snipers . . . we don't know where they are.

Suroosh: But it, but it's time to go now.

Ahmed: I think so.

Suroosh: Why?

01:35:20:25
Ahmed: Because, maybe. I know, I told you because
some of journalist work it's difficult sometimes. So
not all of the times it is free, not all of the times
is safe for them and for the guys that protect the
journalists also.

Ahmed (subtitled): Because, maybe . . . I tell you
because some of journalist's work . . . it's difficult
sometimes. So not all of the times is free, not all of
the times is safe for them and for the guys that protect
the journalists also.

Suroosh: If we, if we stood here for two hours, would
we be kidnapped? Or killed? Where we are right now.

01:35:35:00
Ahmed: If you stayed here for two hours? Maybe the
American come, American army, maybe the IP. They don't
allow us to stay here for more than five minutes only.

Ahmed (subtitled): If you stayed here for two hours?
Maybe the Americans come, the American army, maybe the
IP [Iraqi Police], they don't allow us to stay here for
more than five minutes only.

Suroosh: So it's dangerous?

Ahmed: It's danger. Yeah.

Ahmed (subtitled): It's danger. Yeah.

Suroosh: Let's move on.

01:35:56:06
[Int. car, shots of Baghdad from car]

01:36:00:00
Ahmed: Yeah, they follow us.

Ahmed (subtitled): Yeah, they follow us.

Eddy (off-camera): They're following us.

Narration: Turns out Ahmed was right; as soon as we left
we were stopped by Iraqi Police cars. The problem is
that there, nobody knows who they can trust. What looks
like Iraqi Police might actually be a private militia.
They get the cars, the uniforms, and the guns, and then
they go out on their own and they turn into vigilante
madmen. At that point, we really tested the limits of
our security guys. They put us back in the cars, they
took us back to the hotel, and that's when we knew what
our boundaries were, 'cause our Iraqi bodyguards, who
live in Baghdad, were now bad tripping.

01:36:38:27
TEXT ON SCREEN:
IRAQI POLICE

01:36:41:14
[Int. hotel]

Suroosh: This is our, our, our *Vice* company lunch
today. It's our, uh, our militia. We pushed the limit
with them, they got pissed off, they had enough of our

bullshit. So we're buying them kebabs to cheer them up,
to appease them. I think it's working.

01:37:00:00
[Ext. hotel]

Narration: Our security company was confused by the
nature of our mission. Their mandate was to protect
us at all costs, so as the days went on they just kept
adding more and more guards to our detail.

Suroosh: We've got twelve shooters.

Security (some off-camera): [Speaks in Arabic.]

Suroosh: Do you feel safe?

Eddy (off-camera): No.

Suroosh: Eddy.

Eddy (off-camera): No.

Suroosh: Eddy. Look to my side.

Eddy (off-camera): I don't.

Suroosh: You don't?

Eddy (off-camera): No.

Narration: On the Friday of that week, we convinced
Firas to come meet us at our hotel, the Al-Mansour, and
he also brought Faisal, the lead singer, with him.

[Int. restaurant in hotel]

01:37:29:12
TEXT ON SCREEN:
FAISAL

Narration: They are best friends who live fifteen minutes away from each other and they haven't seen each other in six months. That's a sign of how bad things are in Baghdad, that people who are really close to each other won't take the risk to see one another for fear of losing your lives and taking unnecessary trips out into the street.

01:37:53:24
[Int. hotel room, shots of Baghdad from balcony]

Suroosh: What do you think when you look out our window, and you see, you know, Baghdad, from this perspective, does it, has it changed much? Does it look different?

Firas: I mean, look at it from the top of Baghdad, you would say everything just simple, and easy, just a regular life, people walking, cars goes by and everything just normal. Once you get downstairs . . .

[Shot of people from car]

Firas (cont'd): . . . and talk to people, or just walk with them, or whatever, you [are] just like in a dream and you, then you go to a nightmare.

[Shot of mangled buildings from car]

Firas (cont'd): The problem is you can't wake up, you know what I'm saying?

Suroosh: Are you guys surprised that you're still alive?

Firas (off-camera): Oh, yeah, dude.

Faisal: It's so amazing that we [are] still talking and breathing and eat and laughing sometimes.

Suroosh: So where are the other guys from the band? Are they around?

Firas: The guys left. It's just me and the lead vocals, Faisal. Tony, he's in Syria.

01:38:34:00
[Archival: Footage of Tony playing guitar]

TEXT ON SCREEN:
TONY

Firas (cont'd): He been there for a year, working, I mean, trying to support his family, and also finding a good place for his band just to go to and start their new beginning there.

01:38:43:00
[Archival: Footage of Marwan playing drums]

TEXT ON SCREEN:
MARWAN

Firas: Marwan, he just went to Syria about like couple months ago just to help Tony doing the same thing.

01:38:48:00
[Archival: Footage of Ahmed playing guitar at 2005 Al-Fanar Hotel concert]

TEXT ON SCREEN:
AHMED

Firas: Ahmed, he's in Jordan. He was temporary new member of the band. He was in with us, last concert we did with you guys, by help of *Vice*.

01:38:56:00
[Archival: Footage of fans]

Firas: These are our fans and most of them [are] either dead or out of this country. The rest are, we don't know about them anything. They just, they just disappeared, you know. And now we, we are thinking about, I mean going there, follow others to Syria and we hope we can make it, yeah.

01:39:14:00
[Archival: Footage of band playing concert]

Suroosh (off-camera): Why don't you tell us a bit about the concerts that you've played since the band started?

Firas: In total, we made six, six shows, yeah, and in five years or five and a half years we made six shows.

01:39:23:00
[Archival: Photo of first concert]

Firas: The first concert was in 2002, in the summer 2002.

Faisal: It was the first time we get on the stage. We were so confused and so nervous.

Firas: Actually it was a great show. Everybody enjoyed it and it was fun, dude. And, this is from the fourth concert . . .

01:39:36:00
[Archival: Photo from fourth concert]

Firas (cont'd): . . . 2003, before the war, and was so much pressure because of the war, you know that was coming and everything.

01:39:46:00
[Archival: Photo of the band from fourth concert]

Firas (cont'd): It was a great concert and a lot of people attended and we made a cover song for Slayer . . .

01:39:48:00
[Archival: Photo of bassist playing at concert]

Firas (cont'd): . . . and everybody just fucking start,
you know, headbanging. They broke the chairs and they . . .
they tore up the whole place, dude, this was a big mess.

Faisal: Some of them was, were drunk and was bringing
bottles of whiskey, and . . .

Firas: What the fans used to do is go to the bathroom,
get a couple shots of the drink, and threw the bottle
in the bathroom and come back to the concert. It was so
funny, dude. It was awesome.

Faisal: Those were very great days.

01:40:14:00
[Archival: Footage of band playing concert at Al-Sayed
Hunting Club, 2003]

TEXT ON SCREEN:
AL-SAYED HUNTING CLUB, 2003
UDAY HUSSEIN'S FORMER PARTY SPOT

Firas (off-camera): 2003 was a like a youth festival.
They invited us to go play there. We played like, I don't
know, like three, four songs. And basically we got kicked
out of the stage because people started doing headbanging
and shit like that. They were so happy, dude. It was the
only way they could express their anger, you know, just
by shaking their heads, get all crazy.

Suroosh (off-camera): Things have really changed since
then.

Firas (off-camera): Yeah, of course, of course.

Suroosh (off-camera): A festival, you're invited to
play, everything was relatively peaceful.

01:40:42:00
[Archival: Footage of 2005 concert at Al-Fanar Hotel]

247

TEXT ON SCREEN:
AL-FANAR HOTEL, 2005

Suroosh (off-camera, cont'd): And then a year later,
we did our concert with you, which was very difficult
to pull off. Cut to today, and you can't even walk
down the street.

Firas: Yeah, I mean, we haven't jam[med] onstage
since the concert that we made with you guys, so
almost it's been a year now, and . . . it sucks, dude.
Because I mean, it's basically, okay, we're talking
here about a free country, right, which is now Iraq,
which has become a free country, okay? Where's the
freedom if I can't wear what I want, if I can't say
what I want, if I fucking wear what I want? Where's
the freedom here?

01:41:18:22
[Ext. hotel by pool]

Firas (cont'd): After that last show, I mean, we hadn't
seen each other maybe for last five months. I mean.

Faisal: I mean, we used to train about twelve hours a
day and six hours a day. See, um, here we . . .

Eddy (off-camera): What do you think, there's these
fucking idiots swimming in the pool, laps over here,
and there's guns going off over there, and there's guns
going off over there. What, what's going on?

Firas: That's all right. It's part of the life.

Faisal: It's a bunch of chaos. I mean, you can't explain
that even thousand years.

Suroosh: You guys were talking about practicing. Do you
rehearse a lot? You have a practice space, right?

248

Firas: The first few weeks we started, before the first concert, we didn't rehearse and they're like practicing or rehearsing there for like twenty-one hours a day.

01:41:57:25
[Archival: Footage of band playing in practice space, November 2003]

TEXT ON SCREEN:
PRACTICE SPACE
NOVEMBER 2003

Firas (cont'd): Sometimes we eat and sleep in this fucking place and you sit there and fucking rehearse and keep playing and playing and playing.

Faisal: You don't get bored, you don't get sick of it.

Suroosh (off-camera): You mentioned that something happened to your practice space. Can you tell us what happened to it?

Firas: What happened, I was sitting in my house, you know, just like a regular, uh, just like a regular day, and early in the morning like around nine o'clock, nine, nine thirty, ten o'clock, something like that, you know, we heard all the fucking bombing shit, it was like about fifteen to seventeen explosion. Everybody's fucking freaked out, you know, trucks is running forward and backward, fire trucks, police, man, all kind of fucking forces and you know, like I didn't care because I didn't knew that was my store or my fucking garage that got blowed up or the building itself. So I set home, nobody shows up anything on the news, nothing on the news. And then Faisal called me, he told me, "Hey, you know what? The building got fucking hit by a rocket." I said, "Dude, I mean, are you serious?" He said, "Yeah, I mean, you go check it," I mean.

Suroosh: So the store was actually the practice space.

Firas, Faisal (off-camera): Yeah.

Firas: This, uh, this practice space we lost, I mean it was like all we got, I mean it's not anymore, we can't really afford—

[Sound of gunshots]

Firas (cont'd): Hey, dude, what's up? We can't really afford another, like, practice space.

Faisal: I think, I think it's time to go, dude. I mean, sorry, but it's getting late and uh . . .

Suroosh: So can you explain why you have to cut it short right now? What happens over the next couple hours?

Faisal: Because of all of that shit. Because of all of that shit. You have to be smart enough to go back home at five or six o'clock and that—six o'clock, and that will be the minimum time to you, for your hanging around outside. Can we go now?

01:43:43:12
[Fade to black]

[Instrumental rock music starts]

[Shots of ext. car]

01:43:44:10
[Int. car, driving]

Suroosh (off-camera): So we're going to the practice space right now. This is the place that the band described as where they would go to escape from this life, and it got hit by a Scud missile, or something. And they lost everything, their amps, their guitars, their basses. So we're gonna call Firas and ask him to meet us there. They're very, very nervous about it. They don't want to get seen with us.

01:43:11
Ahmed: This is danger here, you cannot walk here.

Ahmed (subtitled): This is danger here. You cannot walk here.

Eddy (off-camera): No?

01:44:12:23
Ahmed: It's a little danger, not very, very danger. But you can meet him at the hotel.

Ahmed (subtitled): It's a little danger, not very, very danger . . . but you can meet them at the hotel.

01:44:22:20
[Int. car, stopped at checkpoint]

Suroosh: So getting anything done is really hard, uh, we're just trying to get to the practice space, but so far it's not going so well, and just being out here is really tense. The streets are blocked off . . . I just want to go see a practice space, is that so much to ask for?

[Firas walks back toward the car after speaking with guards]

Suroosh (off-camera): Hey, here he is. What's up, man?

01:44:39:28
Firas: Hey, what the hell, dude. I mean.

Firas (subtitled): Hey, what the hell, dude. I mean . . .

Suroosh: Too many people? We didn't know they were gonna come with so . . .

Suroosh (subtitled): Too many people? We didn't know they were gone come with so . . .

Firas: Too many people, the street is blocked. The building itself is locked, but anyway, I got it all on, on video on these CDs.

Firas (subtitled): Too many people, the street is blocked . . . the building itself is locked . . . but anyway . . . I got it all on . . . on video on these CDs.

Suroosh: Okay, okay, great.

Firas: And I will describe everything to you.

Suroosh: Great. You want to come with us?

Firas: Of course, after people see me talking to you, like, I mean, you know, you look shady, you have a shady car.

Suroosh: So why don't you just get in with us?

Firas: Yeah, that's what I'm [inaudible, laughing] . . .

01:45:04:00
[Int. car, driving, shots of street]

01:45:08:16
Eddy (off-camera): See, there's a guitar shop.

Eddy (subtitled): See, there's a guitar shop.

Firas (off-camera): Yeah, there is a guitar shop, and it's all closed because they got threatening for selling guitars.

Eddy (off-camera): No.

Firas (off-camera): Yeah, dude, believe it.

[Shot of demolished building]

Firas (off-camera): Okay, this is Karadah Street, as you
see. This building got bombed on the same day that our
buildings got bombed.

[Driving past former practice space]

Firas (off-camera): If you look to the left side,
right here, you see this is the gate of the building,
this is the alleyway, you could shoot it through the
alleyway, you could see the damage that happened to
the building. Now, look, keep looking, look through the
alleyway.

Eddy (off-camera): Oh yeah, there it is.

Firas: Here is where the rocket hits.

01:45:43:15
[Int. cafe, Suroosh and Firas talking]

Suroosh: So you don't even have a bass anymore, your
bass got destroyed?

Firas: It got fucking totally destroyed. See, that's
what left of it.

[Shows image on cellphone]

Firas: I had to dig for days in the fucking rubbish and
shit to get what left of it.

Suroosh (off-camera): Wow.

01:45:58:07
[Archival: Practice space building after bombing]

01:46:01:16
[Int. hotel room, watching footage on laptop]

253

Firas: This is a video we made about the building
after it fucking got bombed, and we made the video
after two days because the building was kind of
concealed by the police and people, you know, like
trying to get the dead bodies out. That's just the
first floor, I mean the underground floor which is
the basement where we used to rehearse and used to be
our practice space.

01:46:23:06
[Archival: Practice space building before bombing]

01:46:34:06
[Back to postbombing footage]

Faisal: This is where the rocket came from, it's
hitted the building from the side. It was a rocket,
it wasn't something small, it was really big.

Firas: Some people believe that Americans shot it, like
an airplane or like a chopper, rocket, or something.

Faisal: Missiles has been created for wars, for
destroying enemies' bases and territories.

Firas (off-camera): Even if they do have a war this is
not a war zone.

Faisal: This is not a war, this—

Firas: This is a fucking civilian zone, where the
fucking rocket landed, this is just a civilian building
with fucking stores and clinics and, and shit like that.

Suroosh (off-camera): How many times have you watched
this?

Firas: The tape? Basically I watch it daily. You know,
to keep my fucking anger growing, you know. Because,
I'm fucking pissed off, dude. I'm fucking . . . I

don't know what to do, I mean just like I'm totally
ready to do something. It's hard but we got nothing
to do about it, you know. We have to live with it.
You can't tell nobody—who you gonna tell? Anybody
would give a fuck? No. 'Cause it's not their matter,
it's your fucking personal issue. You have to deal
with it every day. Anybody from outside Iraq, nobody
could live under the same circumstances that an Iraqi
could live in. I mean, nobody could live with death,
every day.

Faisal: No matter who you are, no matter what you
are, no matter what shape you are, you are just fighting
for your life, fighting for your own sake. You just
want to do something and nothing in your hands to do.
Just feel like you wanna explode up or something.

Firas: I bet you can find more suicidal motherfuckers
out there in the streets, more than anywhere in the
world, because of all this fucking disappointing things
that happens every day and day and day and fuckin'
fucked-up routines and shit like that. You know, you
have to deal with the same shit every day, you have to
deal with fucking death and fears every day.

01:48:37:17
[Screen goes black]

01:48:38:00
[Archival: Strobe-effect footage of band playing]

[Middle Eastern music plays]

Suroosh (off-camera): You won't be stopped?

Firas (off-camera): No. I mean nothing could have
stopped us, because . . .

01:48:55:16
[Cut back to int. café]

Firas (cont'd): . . . it's nothing about dreams, it's
nothing about this, it's about us, I mean being there,
you know, we, we alive, I mean. Nobody was expecting
that in Iraq heavy metal could exist, but we did, I
mean, we changed the fact that there was nothing here,
and we started it and we're not gonna stop.

01:49:12:00
[Int. car, shots of Baghdad]

Narration: We left Firas and Faisal behind, and got out
of Baghdad feeling helpless about the situation, but we
told them that, if the band ever got back together, we
would help out any way that we could.

01:49:27:10
[Fade to black]

01:49:29:26
TEXT ON SCREEN:
FOUR MONTHS LATER

01:49:33:20
TEXT ON SCREEN:
DECEMBER 2006

Narration: Four months later, we get an email from
Firas saying that Acrassicauda has gotten back together
and they're all living as heavy metal refugees in
Damascus, Syria.

01:49:38:00
[Ext. Damascus, day]

01:49:38:20
TEXT ON SCREEN:
DAMASCUS, SYRIA

Suroosh: Check, check.

Eddy (off-camera): Great.

Suroosh: We're on.

Eddy (off-camera): We're on.

[Shots of city from car]

Suroosh: The rock 'n' roll refugees are playing
their first show in Damascus since they got out of
Iraq and have reunited with their mates, and, um, we're
gonna go see what heavy metal in Syria is all about.
Let's go, buddy.

**Narration: A month before we went to Damascus, a UN
report came out, it said that . . .**

01:50:22:10
TEXT ON SCREEN:
80% OF ALL IRAQI SINGERS HAVE FLED THE COUNTRY
SOURCE: IRIN-UN

**Narration (cont'd): . . . eighty percent of all Iraqi
singers have fled the country, and at least . . .**

01:50:25:07
TEXT ON SCREEN:
75 SINGERS KILLED IN IRAQ SINCE THE U.S. INVASION
SOURCE: IRIN-UN

**Narration (cont.): . . . seventy-five have been killed
since the U.S. invasion started. And since the fall of
2006 the insurgents have been posting decrees everywhere
that are banning, quote . . .**

01:50:33:17
TEXT ON SCREEN:
"MUSIC-FILLED PARTIES, AND ALL KINDS OF SINGING"
SOURCE: *WASHINGTON POST*

Narration (cont'd): . . . music-filled parties, and all kinds of singing, end quote.

[Int. car; shot of driver]

Suroosh (off-camera): This is Jeremana?

Driver: Yeah, yeah.

Suroosh: Cool. This neighborhood here is where all the Iraqi refugees now live.

01:50:44:14
TEXT ON SCREEN:
JEREMANA, DAMASCUS

Narration: By the time we went to meet these guys in Damascus, the studies that had come out claimed that . . .

01:50:50:13
[Screenshot from washingtonpost.com: "Study Claims Iraq's 'Excess' Death Toll Has Reached 655,000"]

Narration (cont'd): . . . 655,000 Iraqis had died because of the U.S. invasion. But there's another issue that hasn't been reported on in the media as much. It's about the Iraqi exodus. During the last four years, 2.4 million Iraqis have fled their country.

01:51:04:26
[Map with arrows indicating movement of Iraqi refugees to neighboring countries]

Narration (cont'd): About 700,000 of them are in Jordan, 400,000 have fled to other countries in the Middle East, and there are about 1.2 million Iraqi refugees living in Syria.

01:51:13:11
TEXT ON SCREEN:
AS OF DECEMBER 2006
THE U.S. HAS LET IN ONLY 466 IRAQIS

**Narration (cont'd): The United States have let in only
466 Iraqis.**

[Car stops, Firas appears]

01:51:23:20
Suroosh (off-camera): As-Salamu Alaykum.

01:51:26:07
Firas: Salaam.

Suroosh (off-camera): How are you, buddy?

Firas: I'm fine, dude. Let's go.

01:51:30:02
[Ext. Damascus—Suroosh and Firas walking down sidewalk]

Suroosh: It's good to see you, man.

01:51:32:07
Firas: It sucks here.

Firas (subtitled): It sucks here.

Suroosh: Does it? [Laughs] Really?

Firas: Yeah.

Suroosh: You miss home.

Suroosh (to Eddy): Well, all he told me is that it sucks
here, and he misses home, he misses the war zone that he
just escaped from.

259

01:51:44:10
Firas: Yeah, once you, once, yeah, dude, I miss the
fucking bombing and shit like that. It's part of my
life, dude.

Firas (subtitled): Yeah, dude, I miss the fucking
bombing and shit like that. It's part of my life, dude.

Suroosh: Yeah. Is this where you live, in this
neighborhood?

Firas: No, all the, all the—

Suroosh: This is where all the Iraqis live, right?

Firas: Most live here, yeah.

Suroosh: You came with your wife?

01:52:00
Firas: Yeah, I came with my wife and my little baby, kid.

Firas (subtitled): Yeah. I came with my wife and my
little baby.

Suroosh: Wow.

01:52:01:00
[Ext. night—Suroosh and Firas enter building]

01:52:02:16
TEXT ON SCREEN:
CAFÉ VITALITY
POOL HALL/INTERNET CAFÉ

Suroosh (off-camera): When's the last time they had a
concert in this neighborhood?

Firas (off-camera): This is the first one.

260

[Int. walking through halls of Café Vitality]

Suroosh: This is the first one. They've never done a
concert here before.

Firas: No.

Suroosh: It's cool. All right, so who, who do we got here?

Firas (off-camera): This is Faisal.

Suroosh: He grew his hair out.

Faisal: How you doing, man? Uh, Suroosh I want to meet
you with Tony, the lead guitarist of the band.

Suroosh: Hey, hey, really nice to meet you.

Firas: This is Marwan.

Suroosh: How are you, very nice to meet you, Marwan.

Eddy (off-camera): Eddy. How you doing?

Suroosh: Tell me, was it hard to get in—to Syria?

Firas: No.

Bandmate (off-camera): No, no, it wasn't hard, but
the way to Syria. It was dangerous, like robbers and
thieves . . .

Suroosh (off-camera): Oh my God.

Firas: All the way from Baghdad to the Iraqi border,
it was like, like, and the road like three buses got
robbed, totally—I mean, you see the buses stopped
there, nobody there, no people, no clothes, nothing.

Suroosh (off-camera): Oh my God.

Firas: Nothing at all, just the bus by itself, in the middle of the desert.

<u>01:52:41:07</u>
Faisal: We got robbed in the beginning, I mean, from the uh, bus, uh, organizer who bring us here, he took triple the, uh, price from us.

Faisal (subtitled): And we got robbed in the beginning, I mean . . . from the bus organizer who bring us here . . . he took triple the price from us.

Firas: And we were lucky, we made it out.

Suroosh: How long did it take to get from Baghdad to the border?

Firas: Sixteen hours.

Suroosh: So you were freakin' out for sixteen hours?

Firas: Exactly, yeah, I was, I—

Suroosh: And you were together.

Firas: Yeah.

Suroosh: But you did it, you got out, you guys are reunited.

<u>01:53:13:27</u>
Faisal: A year, two years.

Faisal (subtitled): It's been two years.

<u>01:53:16:02</u>
Firas: We gonna do the setup thing.

Firas (subtitled): We are gonna . . . set up things . . .

01:53:19:12
Firas: We, we have to haul ass because we're gonna start around seven o'clock, okay?

Firas (subtitled): We have to haul ass because we're gonna start rehearsing around seven o'clock, okay?

Faisal: 'Scuse us.

01:53:24:21
[Int. Vitality Café, band setting up for show]

[Sound of electric guitars]

[Suroosh leaves to walk around Damascus]

01.:53:32:24
[Ext. Damascus night]

Suroosh: It's nice here in Damascus. No bombs going off. This country's on the State Department's list of countries . . .

01:53:40:17
[Screenshot of: U.S. Department of State website: "State Sponsors of Terrorism"]

Suroosh (cont'd): . . . who sponsor terrorism. It's technically slightly beyond the axis of evil. I think it's good vibes.

01:53:54:16
[Police approach, demanding passports]

01:53:56:19
TEXT ON SCREEN:
POLICE.

TEXT ON SCREEN:
PASSPORT! PASSPORT! PASSPORT! PASSPORT!

Narration: It turns out he was part of Syrian
intelligence. There are guys like that roaming around
Damascus everywhere. They stopped us because of our
camera, and apparently we got off easy.

Suroosh: But I live in New York, and I'm Canadian.

[Officer hands back passport]

01:54:14:10
Suroosh: [speaks in Arabic]

Suroosh (subtitled): Thank you.

Suroosh: I kind of feel like we should go back
downstairs for a while [laughing].

01:54:20:19
[Int. Vitality Café basement]

Narration: I really didn't know what to expect when I
was going to Damascus. We didn't know if it was gonna
be a thousand Syrian metal kids going crazy or if it
was gonna be a total bust, and it was somewhere in
between and closer to the latter. It turns out there
is no metal scene in Damascus. So these guys have moved
there, they're living as refugees, their sole goal in
life is to play heavy metal, and they have no audience
to play to.

Marwan: We're so worried, 'cause like there's not
that much of audience down there. We made a decision,
all four of us, that if the, this concert will make
like, if we make a big gig down here, we'll last
forever, we'll keep playing music, 'cause like the
whole situation are different for us right now, you

know, the economy, the financial thing and stuff, because we are foreigners down here, so, probably this will gonna be the last gig for Acrassicauda.

Suroosh: All right. Here it is. Perhaps the last Acrassicauda concert ever. News to us.

01:55:21:09
[Ext. street outside Vitality, intercut with shots from downstairs]

Suroosh: The concert's gonna happen in about an hour, they're finishing up the setup, and, uh, they're playing mostly, mostly covers tonight because the people here don't know anything about this band. They're gonna ramp up toward playing a set of originals. It's like Iraq was before the war, as far as heavy metal goes, in that people were afraid to support heavy metal because the government equates it with, with Satan worship.

01:55:47:03
[Shot of flyer on ext. wall]

Suroosh (cont'd): So the flyers don't even say "metal" on them, they say "rock 'n' roll" concert or something like that. (Reading flyer) Acrassicauda! Rock! (laughs)

01:56:03:09
[Int. Vitality Café basement; Acrassicauda beginning their set]

[Music]

Narration: The concert basically went from bad to good. It started off with "The Final Countdown" by Europe, which was a real bummer, and then they started playing better covers, they played some Guns N' Roses, and they kind of freaked out when they played Metallica.

Marwan: Okay. This song's called "Fade to Black."

[Band begins song]

Narration: These guys have never had the opportunity
to see Metallica, so suddenly there's a band of Iraqi
guys playing Metallica songs, and they're stoked. For
a moment they're imagining that they're at a Metallica
show and they're all singing along to "Fade to Black"
and "One," and then after that, the crowd had been like
warmed up, and the band decided to play some originals,
and that's when the crowd really got going. And the
band, they kinda killed it at that point, as well.

01:57:59:14
TEXT ON SCREEN
"UNDERWORLD"

[Music]

[Shots of band playing passionately. At end of song
crowd chants:]

Audience (off-camera): A-cra-ssicauda! A-cra-ssicauda!

01:58:13:10
Eddy (off-camera): Are you gonna play again?

Eddy (subtitled): Are you gonna play again?

Marwan: So I'm sorry I have to admit it, and I hate it
when I'm wrong, but Acrassicauda will play again. So
metal up your ass, guys.

01:58:21:07
Marwan (subtitled): So metal up your ass, guys!

Suroosh: They're not breaking up!

Suroosh (subtitled): They're not breaking up!

Marwan: Nope, never! Hey, hope you enjoy it, guys.

Suroosh (off-camera): That was great.

01:58:31:05
[Int. car, driving through Damascus—day]

[Music: Acrassicauda]

Narration: After the concert was over, we were setting up a time the next day for us to meet and Marwan invited us over to have dinner with them. And so we drove out to the outskirts of Damascus up into the hills, where they have these big concrete blocks of flats that look like projects.

[Shots of sand-colored, boxy apartment buildings]

Suroosh: This is where three of the guys live, Marwan came here first, and then Faisal and Firas moved into this building over here. They all live in the basement in three cubes next to one another. There are some Somalis who live upstairs. The building has no heat. Let's go in.

[Suroosh descends stairs into the building]

Narration: Marwan cooked us dinner, it consisted of spaghetti with liver. They were extremely generous with what little they had.

01:59:23:18
[Suroosh knocks on apartment door; shot from int. apartment as he enters]

Narration: And we just got to see what their lives had consisted of since they left Baghdad, it's an incredibly stark existence.

Suroosh: So, last night, if the concert went terribly, and you said we're gonna break up the band, I quit, you know, Acrassicauda's done. What's your option? What would you do?

267

Marwan: I was, I was out of options for the band or like for my life. And like for the first time—my family down there like, calling me—and for the first time my family was really interested about the band and us. 'Cause my family knows as well as I know, and all the guys down here know, that we don't have a better option.

Faisal: When I, when I came here, I took all my, my savings. I mean, I've been spending a lot of money just to make sure that this is my future, okay? And if this band's not going to work, don't ask me about it, I don't know.

Suroosh: Let's just say, in theory, that the band broke up, would you go back to the war zone in Baghdad instead of staying here?

Marwan: Yeah, I was like yeah I'm going back to Baghdad in case this concert fail, I'll go back to Baghdad and face it. Probably like I'll die down there, but like who gives a fuck, man? After all, I'm like we refuse the idea about like from ashes to ashes and dust to dust, I mean, like we wanna be remembered. That's the thing.

02:00:54:02
[Int. apartment, int. car, driving through Damascus at dusk, shots of Damascus at night]

[Music: Heavy metal]

Narration: Just like Firas, Faisal, and Marwan, about three thousand Iraqis continue to flee their country every day. Technically, they're refugees, but they're not refugees in the traditional sense of living in camps . . .

02:01:06:01
[Archival: Photos of refugee camps]

Narration (cont'd): . . . and being malnourished. It's a certain segment of Iraqi society that's getting out.

It's mostly those with education and money. And that's
caused a huge brain drain in Iraq. And once they get to
places like Syria, they're not allowed to work legally.
All this is creating what some organizations are calling
the fastest-growing . . .

02:01:23:09
[Screenshot of Refugees International website]

Narration (cont'd): . . . humanitarian crisis in the
world.

02:01:31:20
[Int. basement apartment]

Suroosh: What's life like as a heavy metal refugee?

Marwan: Oh, bad. This is the place that we're staying
in, this is the place that we had to rehearse for
the first concert in Syria, and it's like three meters
underground, man. I mean, like the situation in Iraq
is getting like bad to worse, like to horrible, and,
and, and like we don't know. I mean, like my family
calls me like every week or something, and telling me,
like don't get back to Iraq, don't get back to Iraq,
the situation is like horrible down here. And I'll be
like, for how long?

Faisal: What I'm, what I'm still not happy about, I
mean, I left my family down there suffering still. I
mean, they, they were supporting me from all sides.
They been telling me, just get out, leave your, uh, live
your life, just go.

Marwan: I'm like, I had like, I worked like a few
jobs, like probably a couple, like three jobs down
here, and now I know how it is like to be a foreign,
an Iraqi person actually, not even like foreign, we're
not even like on the level of the foreigns here, we are
like down the level of the foreigns, 'cause you know,

too many Iraqis down here, like, I guess, like kind of like, the Syrian people is kind of pissed off of having like more Iraqis 'cause all that, like, you know, affecting their economies, and they don't have like a great economy down here. So I went down there and I worked in these like stores like washing dishes and clean up floors, selling like stuff to people and knocking on other like strange people doors and like offer them stuff, and I was like, and they pay you like real low and they're using you most of the time 'cause they, they know that you don't have a better option.

Suroosh: How much were you getting paid per hour?

Marwan: Fuckin'. It's like real shame. I'm like one hundred dollar a month, man. And let's say we're talking about like twelve hours work in a day.

Suroosh: Six days a week?

Marwan: Yeah, and you don't have. No— fi— seven days a week.

Suroosh: It's like you're out of the death and destruction for the first time in years.

Firas: Yeah.

Suroosh: You have a wife and a kid that you brought from Baghdad, as well.

Firas: Yeah.

Suroosh: What's the vibe now, are you guys happy? Life has a, you know.

Firas: It's safer.

Suroosh: Yeah.

Firas: Here, it's safer. But it's not a happy place. I mean, just like what they said, I mean, my friend says before, it's . . . you have to start over again. You have to start building everything from nothing and basically, you got nothing, you're below zero here because in Baghdad you had the zero, you had your friends, you had everything. But here you have nobody except you and your music, so you have to build it up again from nothing at all. I can—because here, as I mean whatever I do, I don't feel like home, you know what I'm saying?

02:04:20:23
[Music]

Narration: We ended up spending about seven hours with these guys in this really, really cold room that had no windows, uh, at the end of the night, they basically said, "We're a band and what we want more than anything in this world is for our record to come out," and they said, "If you guys were serious in your offer to help us, what can we do?" We said, "Look, go out there, find a studio, we'll record some demos and we'll take it from there." So Marwan picked up the phone, started making calls and chasing leads and finding out where you could record a heavy metal record in Damascus.

02:04:55:10
Marwan: [speaks in Arabic]

Marwan (subtitled): Buddy, I need to ask you a question. Is there a studio for recording that you know of? That records songs well? Something good, hopefully.

Suroosh: What did he say?

Marwan: Uh, he says call me in eleven o'clock and I will give you a number for a guy so if we are going to make the first album for Acrassicauda.

271

[Music begins]

[Int. concert in Damascus, ext. on streets of Damascus]

Narration: The night of Acrassicauda's first concert in Damascus, we met a kid named Mike . . .

Mike: What's up, man.

Narration (cont'd): . . . a nineteen-year-old Iraqi refugee who's Acrassicauda's biggest fan. It turns out he's also learning how to play guitar and Tony's his teacher.

Mike: Tony . . . is like a brother for me . . . Maybe I talk to him more than I talk to my brother even. So they are good friends. They are cool.

Narration: Tony is a phenomenal guitar player. At one point in his life he wanted to become a civil engineer but he gave it all up to pursue his dream of playing guitar. He's pretty shy, introverted, doesn't speak a lot of English.

Suroosh: What would happen if somebody said to you, you can't play guitar anymore?

Tony: Ehhhhhh!

Suroosh: Hahaha . . .

Tony: No . . . I can't stop.

Suroosh: You can't stop?

Narration: Tony was the first one to come to Damascus. He came a year before Faisal and Firas . . . and unfortunately, his situation was far more complex than

the other guys in the band. His dad's a drunk and his mom
and his three younger sisters came over to Damascus from
Baghdad, and left his father behind. Now, he had to take
care of all of them so he worked in restaurants, and he
started giving guitar lessons to help pay the bills.

Suroosh: How many students do you have here?

Tony: Uhhh, four.

Narration: As the band was looking around Damascus for
studios to record their demos in, we enlisted Mike.

02:06:39:13
[Int. of car, ext. walking around Damascus, bus station]

Narration: We hired him as our buddy/translator/
gopher. We hired him to take us around different parts
of Damascus to help us understand the Iraqi refugee
situation a little bit better.

Suroosh: This is the bus station where all the cars
come in from Iraq every day. These big gas-guzzling
Suburbans barreling through the desert. They go through
Mosul and Fallujah and it's apparently a real nightmare.
The guys in Acrassicauda, they did this trip. Uh,
they're not letting us shoot here, for some reason.
We have to get permission from Syrian government, so
we're trying to bypass that right now.

Eddy (off-camera): So how do you like it here? How long
have you been here now?

Mike: Seven months.

Suroosh (off-camera): Do you have family back in Iraq?

Mike: Relatives, yeah, in Iraq, yeah. Every Iraqi family
in Iraq lost someone from their relatives or from their
family. Bad things in Iraq, that's why we are here.

Iraqi people don't deserve that, you know? All that
happened to them. It's bad.

02:07:41:07
Mike (subtitled): Iraqi people don't deserve that,
you know? All that happened to them. It's bad.

Suroosh: Do you believe in God?

Mike: Sure, I believe in God but I start like not to
believe in God after what happened in Iraq. Because
where's God, he will support us, right? And what
happened in Iraq? But I thinks that things will get
better, after years, after many Iraqi people die.

02:08:09:22
[Suroosh and Mike walk through the streets over to the
cemetery]

[Music begins: Instrumental]

Eddy (off-camera): So can you, can you tell us where we
are right now?

02:08:18:14
Mike: This is the cemetery of strangers' people who die
here in Syria. So they get buried here.

Mike (subtitled): This is the cemetery of strangers'
people who die here in Syria. So they get buried over
here.

Suroosh: What's interesting about this graveyard is
that these are all graves of Iraqis who were pushed
out of their country and, uh, the bus station is right
over there, it's about a two-minute walk away, so they
get off their buses after getting exiled or running
away from their lives and then they live out their last
years in Syria and then die and get buried just a couple
blocks from where they first came in.

<u>02:08:54:24</u>
[Shots of streets and cars at night from int. of car, int. of car, int. of studio]

Suroosh (cont'd): So we're on our way to the studio. We're trying to record a heavy metal album in Damascus. I'm not sure if it's ever been done before. In the oldest inhabited city in the world, I think that they would have gotten around to recording a heavy metal record at some point.

[Music]

Narration: The studio is in the basement of a house that these two Syrian Christian brothers lived in. They chain-smoked like no one I have ever seen, they'd also never recorded a full band before. They didn't know how to mike a drum kit, they only ever recorded traditional Arab music backed up by shitty synthesizers, but they were up for working together, and at that point we didn't have any other options anyway.

Marwan: As-Salamu Alaykum.

Suroosh: Wa alaikum assalam.

<u>02:09:54:21</u>
Marwan: [speaks in Arabic]

Marwan (subtitled): How are you?

Suroosh: [speaks in Arabic]

Suroosh (subtitled): How are you?

Marwan: [speaks in Arabic]

Marwan (subtitled): Good?

Suroosh: [speaks in Arabic]

Suroosh (subtitled): Good.

Suroosh (laughs): What's it like? Your first time recording, ever.

Faisal: Ever. This shit rocks, man. This shit rocks.

Suroosh: Yeah?

Faisal: I'm really excited man.

02:10:10:25
TEXT ON SCREEN:
"BETWEEN THE ASHES"

[Music]

Narration: These guys walked into the studio totally cold, to say that they were rusty is a bit of an understatement.

Suroosh: What happened?

02:10:24:10
Marwan: Injured finger.

Marwan (subtitled): Injured finger.

Suroosh: Too much drumming?

Firas (off-camera): Yeah, he got blusters.

Firas (subtitled): Yeah, he got blisters.

Marwan: So good.

Marwan (subtitled): Feels so good!

Narration: Where they were living, they couldn't practice because their neighbors were always complaining

about the noise. Not to mention that they had never
even been in a recording studio before and the idea of
recording one instrument at a time was totally foreign
to them and threw them off their game. We just had
a couple days, the clock was tickin', they wanted to
record six songs, and they ended up getting three done.

02:11:05:05
Tony: [speaks in Arabic]

Tony (subtitled): So you mean right there?

Marwan: [speaks in Arabic]

Marwan (subtitled): You almost nailed it. Why did you
stop? Why? Why?

Suroosh: Dude, he's amazing. He's totally out of
control. He's got crazy skills on that guitar.

Marwan: Oh yeah. Yeah.

02:11:21:27
Tony: Thanks, man.

Tony (subtitled): Thanks, man.

Marwan: This is the first time in my life someone tell
me like de-mute your drums. Everyone keep telling me,
mute them as best as you can. As low as you can. Play
as low as you can.

02:11:34:08
Marwan (subtitled): As low as you can. Play as low as
you can.

Marwan: Oh, and what did we found down here? Christmas
presents.

Suroosh: Ahh. Take that shit out.

[Laughter]

Marwan: Oh yeah.

Suroosh (off-camera): All right, so what is all this shit on the ground?

02:11:47:17
Marwan (off-camera): These all kinds of things that I had to put inside the bass drum so people not gonna complain.

Marwan (subtitled): These are all kinds of things that I had to put inside the bass drum so people not gonna complain.

Suroosh (off-camera): What is this?

Marwan: Uh, this is a rubber tie.

Suroosh (off-camera): A jean jacket.

Marwan: Yeah.

Suroosh (off-camera): You just got used to playing your drums like this over the years. You know what? I think it's going to start sounding better now.

Marwan: Uh, hopefully.

02:12:06:12
[Ext. studio night]

Suroosh (off-camera): How do the songs sound that you've recorded so far?

Tony: [speaks in Arabic]

Tony (subtitled): They sound good.

Suroosh (off-camera): Have we mixed yet?

Firas: Uh, two songs done.

Suroosh: They're done.

Firas: We're still working on "Massacre" because it needs a lot of mixing, sound effects and stuff like that, bombing airplanes.

Suroosh: The sounds of war.

Firas: The sounds of war.

02:12:36:08
[Int. studio]

[Music: The band recording]

Eddy (off-camera): What's happening now? What's, what are you . . .

Eddy (subtitled): What's happening now? What's . . .

Faisal: Well, try, we're trying to mi— mix some lead with the ending or finishing of the "Massacre" song. I'm just tell him, that pretend that there's some woman's trying to cry on her child. All that kind of screaming, all that kind of . . .

Faisal (subtitled): We are trying to mix some lead with the ending, or the finishing of the "Massacre" song. Just . . . pretend that there's some woman trying to cry on her child. All that kind of screaming, all that kind of . . .

Suroosh (off-camera): Here?

Suroosh (subtitled): Right here?

Faisal: Exactly.

Faisal (subtitled): Exactly.

02:13:08:27
Firas: "Massacre" is a song talking about the war since
whenever and you're gonna hear it in the lyrics.

Firas (subtitled): "Massacre" is a song talking about
the war . . . since whenever. And you are gonna hear it
in the lyrics.

02:13:16:02
[Music: "Massacre," sung in Arabic]

"Massacre" lyrics (subtitled): Years ago . . . they
created a new way to kill innocent people. The children,
the elders, and the women. Bombs dropped like rain
from the sky. The rivers are filled with the blood of
the innocent.

[Music: Lyrics end, instrumental still plays]

**Narration: Against all odds, these guys managed to go
into the studio and record three songs, "Underworld,"
"Between the Ashes," and "Massacre." Or, as they like
to call it, "Ma-soccer." And though they were far
from perfect, their mission to record these demos in
Damascus was accomplished.**

Marwan: It's been like amazing, like three days or four
days, man. Like for the first time, like I'm coming back
from studio feel like I done something today.

[Music ends]

02:14:14:01
[Shots of Damascus from car]

[Music begins: Instrumental]

Suroosh: If you think about bands in the West,
bands in Brooklyn where our office is, they're all
so spoiled compared to Acrassicauda. In fact, we're
all spoiled compared to these guys. Now that we've had
a chance to spend time with them and see them in their
homeland . . .

02:14:41:06
[Shot from balcony in Baghdad]

TEXT ON SCREEN:
BAGHDAD, IRAQ
AUGUST 2006

Suroosh (cont'd): . . . and then see them here . . .

02:14:43:22
[Shot of band outside studio]

TEXT ON SCREEN:
DAMASCUS, SYRIA
DECEMBER 2006

Suroosh (cont'd): . . . and the things that they go
through. You know, Marwan is twenty-three years old and
when I talk to him, I feel like I'm talking to someone
who is wiser and older than me. Even though he's, he's
fourteen years younger than me. It's kind of incredible.
They've evolved fast. They've been through war.

02:15:03:26
[Int. of hotel room in Damascus]

**Narration: We went back to our hotel room in central
Damascus. The guys raided the mini-bar and they got a
bit bombed.**

Suroosh: You guys made a record today.

Firas (off-camera): Yeah.

Suroosh: It's the first heavy metal record to ever be recorded . . .

Firas: For an Iraqi band.

Suroosh: . . . for an Iraqi band.

Firas: [laughter]

Faisal: It's kind of impossible. Fuck.

Marwan: In fuckin' thirty hours, man. I done three kick-ass song, man. And like, I'll gonna be happy for like the rest of my life, dude. I'll gonna tell my kids if I ever had one of those fuckers.

02:15:37:23
Firas: What's, what's going on inside of our minds, you know, thinking about home and stuff like that. It doesn't give us even the will to celebrate or do anything else. I got a phone call for today from my mom, says, "Never come back."

Firas (subtitled): What's . . . what's going on inside of our minds, you know, thinking about home and stuff like that. It doesn't give us even the will to celebrate or do anything else. I got a phone call today from my mom. She said, "Never come back."

Suroosh (off-camera): Today?

Firas: Yeah, while I was, I was at the studio.

And she said, "Never come back, try your best to just stay there as much as possible."

Marwan: I got three members of my family down there. Just like, I feel terribly guilty, sad, desperate, and I want to get them the hell outta there. Just like, there ain't safe down there, man. Now it's like

282

there's people like fighting in wars, there's people
like killing injuries, there's people like fixing
stuff, there's people building stuff and I'm making
music. Rock on.

02:16:31:17
[Shots of Damascus from car, int. car]

Narration: What we witnessed in Syria was, for lack
of a better way to put it, the consequence of this
war. What happens when the Americans invade Iraq, it
displaces millions of Iraqis and then they go live as
refugees in other countries.

Suroosh: As Firas said yesterday, they're less than
zero right now. In Baghdad, they knew what zero was.

02:16:51:27
[Shots of Mike in Damascus, at concert, at cemetery]

Narration: As for Mike, who's nineteen, he's probably
got more hope than all of them combined. But he's stuck,
he's in that Syrian purgatory, and there doesn't seem
to be any way out for him right now.

02:17:01:21
Mike: I was just wondering, why we can't like travel?

Mike (subtitled): I was wondering why we can't like
travel.

02:17:04:18
[Int. room]

Mike: Just because we are Iraqi? I want ask someone
to answer me like a government, or like America, why
it's hard like to go to America or to Europe. Just
like for being Iraqi? That's not fair. Is this crime
that I'm Iraqi? Do they think that all Iraqi people are
terrorists? That's insane. Just like want to travel,

want to be free. Like you, dude. You can go any place that you want. I wish if I can like fly. I would go to any place that I want that I feel I comfortable in and that I belong to and do what I want to do and be free.

Mike (subtitled): Just because we are Iraqi? I want to ask someone to answer me . . . like . . . like a government . . . or like America. Why it's hard like to go to America or to Europe . . . just like for being Iraqi? That's not fair. Is it a crime that I'm Iraqi? Do they think that all Iraqi people are terrorists? That's insane. I just want to travel. I want to be free. Like you, dude. You can go any place that you want. I wish I can like fly. I would go to any place that I want . . . that I feel that I'm comfortable in, and that I belong to . . . and do what I want to do . . . be free.

02:17:47:20
[Ext. hotel in Damascus, int. car]

Narration: Before we left Damascus to come back to New York, the guys from Acrassicauda asked us if they could watch some of the footage that we'd shot in Baghdad. So we went back to their place and showed them a rough cut of what we had shot over the last few years.

02:18:03:04
[Int. band apartment, shots of footage from Baghdad on TV]

Suroosh (on the TV): We're in Baghdad, we're here to interview the only Iraqi heavy metal band Acrassicauda . . .

Firas (off-camera): Oop, that's us.

Suroosh (on the TV): We've been following them for three years and, um, we needed to check in on them, see if they're still alive.

02:18:21:20
Marwan: (laughter) I don't know which guy can be
so fucking dumb to name a band like this. Fucking
Latin. It's just like me pronouncing "Mississippi" or
something, man. Fuck, man, I miss Baghdad. I miss Iraq
is what I meant.

Marwan (subtitled): I don't know which guy can be
so fucking dumb to name a band like this. Fucking
Latin! It's just like me pronouncing "Mississippi" or
something, man. Fuck, man, I miss Baghdad. I miss Iraq
is what I meant.

Firas: We were, we are watching just like we are
watching other bands' movies. You know?

Firas (subtitled): We are watching just like we are
watching other bands' movies. You know?

Marwan (off-camera): Yeah, exactly. This is fucking
awesome. The old good days, man.

02:19:04:14
Marwan (subtitled): The old good days, man.

**Narration: It started off really fun. They were seeing
footage of themselves playing these concerts. Hanging
out in Baghdad over the years, but for Marwan, it was
the first time he saw footage of their old practice
space, which had been bombed since he moved to Damascus.**

Marwan: For six years, man. We'd been like bounded to
this store, man. That's, that's.

Faisal (on the TV): (inaudible) This is where the rocket
came from, it's hitted the building from the side. It was
a rocket, it wasn't something small, it was really big.

Firas (on the TV): Some people believe that Americans
shot it. It's hard but we got nothing to do about

285

it, you know? We have to live with it. You can't tell
nobody—who you gonna to tell? Anybody would give a
fuck? No. 'Cause it's not their matter, it's your
fucking personal issue. You have to deal with it every
day. Anybody from outside Iraq, nobody could live under
the same circumstances that an Iraqi could live in. You
know, you have to deal with the same shit every day, you
have to deal with fucking death and fears every day.

02:20:32:03
Firas: It's over, right?

Firas (subtitled): It's over, right?

Suroosh (off-camera): This is the material so far.

Suroosh (subtitled): This is the material so far.

Eddy (off-camera): Till now.

02:20:30:00
Firas (off-camera): Till now. Yeah, shit. Dude, you
got me in the mood. Shit. Aw, man. I remember all that
shit, dude.

Firas (subtitled): Till now, yeah. Dude, you got me in
the mood. Shit. I remember all that shit, dude.

02:20:58:16
Marwan: This is a quite interesting movie that you filmed
down there. You know what? We feel sad. We feel terribly
fucking sad. This is fucking sad scenes. Tragedy scenes.
Seeing the country that you grew up in and all the
people that you know. That don't live anymore. Right
now dead. But you know? These are things that you lay
your back on. These are things that you turn off the
TV whenever or like change the channel when it's on. So
for you fuckers down there, this is how it goes, this
is the daily life in Iraq. This goes to all of you,
fuckers. Pigs.

Marwan (subtitled): This is a quite interesting movie
that you filmed down there. You know what? We feel sad.
We feel terribly fucking sad. This is the fucking sad
scenes. Tragedy scenes. Seeing the country that you grew
up in and all the people that you know. That don't live
anymore. Right now dead. These are things that you lay
your back on. These are things that you turn off the TV
whenever, or like change the channel when it's on. So
for you fuckers down there, this is how it goes, this is
the daily life in Iraq . . . This goes to all of you,
fuckers! Pigs.

02:21:47:09
TEXT ON SCREEN:

SIX MONTHS LATER,
FIRAS, MARWAN, AND FAISAL
HAD NO OPTION BUT TO SELL THEIR INSTRUMENTS
TO PAY THE RENT.

THE SYRIAN GOVERNMENT HAS BEEN TRYING
TO SEND REFUGEES BACK TO IRAQ,
INCLUDING MIKE AND THE MEMBERS
OF ACRASSICAUDA.

TO DATE, ALL OF THEIR ATTEMPTS
TO OBTAIN FOREIGN VISAS HAVE BEEN DENIED.

THE BAND IS STILL TRYING TO
FIND ITS WAY TO A PLACE
WHERE THEY CAN LIVE IN PEACE,
GROW THEIR HAIR LONG,
BANG THEIR HEADS, AND PLAY HEAVY METAL AGAIN
AS LOUD AS THEY WANT.

ACKNOWLEDGMENTS

Thanks to Acrassicauda and their families. *Vice* magazine, VBS, Suroosh Alvi, Eddy Moretti, Shane Smith, Spike Jonze, Brian Orce, Monica Hampton, Andrew Creighton, Tim Small, Bernardo Loyola, John Martin, Cengiz Tanc, Jamie Farkas, Gideon Yago, Waleed Rabia, James Hetfield, Metallica, Alex Skolnick, Testament, Josh Homme, Scott Kelly, Laurent C. Lebec, Brann Dailor, Joe Trohman, Sue Tropio, Christopher Roberts, Rocco Castoro, Ahmet Polat, Raj Karia, Jayantilal Karia, Neil Thomson, Stuart Griffiths, Janos Marton, Ed Zipco, Matt "Maker" Jones, Matt Schoen, and Matthew Heckart.

Acrassicauda would like to thank our families and friends for their support and patience. *Vice* for being crazy enough to gamble everything just to get us here and for keeping the faith. Saad Zai for being such a good teacher and mentor. Mr. Alex Skolnick for his continued support and his great musical knowledge. Mr. James Hetfield for his generosity and support. Cengiz Tanc for being our friend and guardian in Turkey.

We would also like to thank the bands Metallica and Testament for bringing the images of rock 'n' roll into our heads. Also, all the people and bands that helped and participated in the book.

For everyone who helped along the journey from Baghdad to Syria to Turkey and all the way to the States. For the memory of our beloved ones, we will never forget you.

And finally, this book is also for those who refused to give up their dreams and never took the music for granted. We know we are not the only ones.

Marwan: To my dad for teaching me to stand up for what I believe, to my mom for being my home, sanctuary, and shelter, and to my sisters, I'll see you again. To my cousin Mazin, for believing in me and being so patient, I'll pay for the rest of the drums someday. To Baghdad, you'll always be beautiful, this is how we will remember you. To my friends who stood beside me for better or worse, hopefully one day I'll be able to repay you.

Firas: To my parents, for raising me in a way that I am able to see what's right and wrong, and for giving me their support no matter what. I hope that you are proud of me now. Dad, sorry I didn't become a vet. Mom, I love you so much. To my brother and sister, who basically showed me the way in the first place, and taught me to love rock. Wish you were here. To the friends and fans and all the people, thank you for always believing in us and giving us your support.

Tony: First of all, thanks to God. I would like to thank the other band members, my family for their support and for caring for me so much, and all the people who helped us and supported us.

Faisal: For God, who has been giving me the strength to keep going forward, for my parents who never gave up on me, for my big brother and little sister who always believed in me from the very beginning.

Printed in the United States
By Bookmasters